Much Depends On Dinner

First published in Great Britain by

Simon & Schuster UK Ltd, 2008

A CBS Company

Recipes copyright © 2008 the Contributors.

Text and compilation copyright © 2008 Carolyn Hart

All rights reserved.

Simon & Schuster UK Ltd

Africa House, 64–78 Kingsway, London WC2B 6AH

This book is copyright under the Berne Convention.

No reproduction without permission

All rights reserved.

The right of Carolyn Hart to be identified as the Author

of this Work has been asserted by her in accordance with

sections 77 and 78 of the Copyright, Designs and Patents

Act, 1988.

1 3 5 7 9 10 8 6 4 2

Design: Jane Humphrey

Printed and bound in China

ISBN 978-1-84737-051-8

Telegraph Magazine food photography commissioned by
Cheryl Newman, Photography Director, and Krishna Sheth

With special thanks to:

Fabio Diu

Sophie Hart-Walsh

Summer Nocon

Morven Knowles

Cheryl Newman

Much Depends On Dinner

A year in the **Telegraph** kitchen

EDITED BY CAROLYN HART

SIMON & SCHUSTER
A CBS COMPANY

As all generals, wives and mothers know, and Lord Byron astutely pointed out, much depends on dinner – marital sanity, for one thing... Humanity marches on its stomach, whether into battle or into a domestic fracas, and those in charge of the kitchen have the power to seduce and enliven as much as they do to enrage and depress. Over the last three or four years, the Food pages of the *Telegraph Magazine* have endeavoured to promote seduction rather than depression via a collection of recipes that should enable the resident cook to soothe with delicious, sustaining, fresh, seasonal meals, easily and, above all, quickly. It's no good publishing recipes that make you want to reach for the bottle before you've read to the end of the ingredients list, so *Telegraph* recipes are on the short side and notable for their accessibility – which does not in any way compromise their taste or sophistication (locally produced, organic food is at the top of our list). That we've been able to produce such recipes every week for nearly half a decade is entirely due to the generosity and inspirational skills of our many guest cooks (some of them Michelin starred, many of them celebrities or home cooks growing and cooking their own food, all of them happy) nearly 80 of whom are represented here, the talent behind this collection of over 200 recipes.

Contents

What defines a great recipe?   6

Spring   **9**
Salads   10
Eggs   17
Soups   20
Fish and Shellfish   25
Vegetables   33
Meat, Poultry and Game   38
Puddings   46

Summer   **55**
Breakfasts   56
Starters and Al Fresco Lunches   57
Soups   65
Salads   69
Pasta and Rice   79
Fish and Shellfish   81
Meat, Poultry and Game   90
Vegetables   98
Sauces   102
Puddings   104
Afternoon Tea   113

Autumn   **117**
Soups   118
Starters and Light Lunches   123
Fish and Shellfish   130
Meat, Poultry and Game   134
Vegetables   146
Puddings   154
Baking   161

Winter   **165**
Soups   166
Fish and Shellfish   168
Meat, Poultry and Game   171
Vegetables   188
Puddings   193
Chocolate   197
Marmalade   199
Breads   200

Conversion table   *203*
Suppliers   *204*
Index   *205*

Is it the ingenuity in the technique or the scale of the creativity? Both things are necessary yet they fall behind the most essential element, the evocation of seasonality and emotion.

Good cooks have an extra sense that tells them what others would like to eat at a particular time. They are barometers that observe the seasons and scan changes in the weather; they scour the locality for ingredients that give a dish geographical index and then finally they choose what to cook in harmony with all this. The certain result is a plate of food that will stay forever in the memory of the person who eats it.

What defin

Our individual histories are strung together with meals and their emotional connections. Awful or delicious, we remember their smells and textures, relating these recipes to the person who cooked them, the people who were there, the place and the event, no matter how insignificant. Our hearts lie close to our guts – it is not a coincidence that emotion is often felt first as a pang in the stomach...

This book is a collection of great recipes. They have been chosen by *Telegraph Magazine* food editor Carolyn Hart chiefly for their seasonality, but also for their possibilities, the anticipation that the chosen ingredients will produce a drama of wonderful taste. Usual, everyday ingredients used in unusual ways, unusual and extraordinary ingredients used in ordinary, simple ways. They have been taken from a huge archive of articles that have appeared in the magazine since the launch of the Food pages in 2003. The style of these pages follow that of the magazine: intensely curious, newsworthy, well-travelled and sometimes glamorous.

Because many recipes are accompanied by a story about the chef or author of the recipe, about the production of a certain ingredient or the feast itself, each dish in this collection has a definite, sound reason-to-be. The concept and chosen ingredients are part of the story, not just another way with a chicken fillet, not just another excuse to slosh over the chilli and lime marinade and take a picture.

Thomas Keller's roast chicken recipe is a master class that mixes the scientific methodology you would expect from the Californian perfectionist with that hard-to-achieve basic: simplicity. The result is perfectly roasted chicken, how you get there is the story.

Locality is a theme in many of the recipes, no more so than in a dish of Fenland celery, Cambridgeshire potatoes and freshwater Wiltshire crayfish; the mini lobster look-a-likes that have invaded British streams. Taking regional food to its most luxurious limits on other shores, cooks at Krug's Clos de Mesnil vineyard make a tarte aux raisins with the same grapes they crush to make their champagnes. Singed from the oven, the thin skins of the grapes bursting in places, this is a recipe that begs to be made. But humbler dishes beckon. Cooks in a local Aubrac restaurant whip up the flesh of boiled potato with Laguiole cheese to make aligot, a gloop that can compete with the best of British stodge, while fashion designer Luisa Beccaria's pasta with sardines, breadcrumbs and chilli both warms and thrills the belly.

This lovely collection takes enjoyment for granted. Hart admits she is unable to eat the crab crostini on page 58 without an icy drink in hand. Follow her, on this journey to meet the world's most imaginative cooks. Seek out the suggested ingredients and reach for knife and pan. The adventure begins.

Rose Prince

Spring

(MARCH, APRIL, MAY)

'It was that period in the vernal quarter when we may suppose the Dryads to be waking for the season. The vegetable world begins to move and swell and the saps to rise, till in the completest silence of lone gardens and trackless plantations, where everything seems helpless and still after the bond and slavery of frost, there are bustlings, strainings, united thrusts, and pulls-all-together, in comparison with which the powerful tugs of cranes and pulleys in a noisy city are but pigmy efforts.'

Thomas Hardy 1840–1928: 'Far From The Madding Crowd'

Thomas Hardy's rather sexy reflections on the power of spring will strike an empathetic chord with anyone who has spent the last few months labouring in the kitchen to produce what seemed then like the most seductive and deliciously warming fare, but now feels like the restraining folds of a thick brown blanket of stew, casserole and winter pies. Like the Dryads throwing off their winter threads and taking on the vernal green, you want to do a little bustling, straining and thrusting yourself – and chiefly in the direction of the vegetable garden, where the buds are breaking and the March winds waking. In other words, get out there and into a salad. Leaves – watercress, lamb's lettuce, rocket – just a garnish in winter, make meals in themselves now, revitalising the sinews and deslugging the blood. The food of spring is all to do with renewal: eggs, fish, spring lamb, the first asparagus shoots, watercress and spider crabs. Rose Prince, Raymond Blanc, Charlie Trotter, Ferran Adrià, Heston Blumenthal and Michel Roux Jr have all got ways of making the sap rise...

Salads
Rocket, mint, beetroot and feta salad with olive oil and lemon juice dressing
SERVES 4-6

Sarah Raven's salad has lots of different flavours – 'the heat of the rocket, the sweetness of the fresh beetroot and mint and the saltiness of the feta. It is a lovely combination on its own, as a first course, and only takes five minutes to make. It's also good with duck and game. For a summer lunch or first course, the beetroot can be substituted with cubes of watermelon, and in the autumn you can replace the beetroot with roasted squash.'

4 medium-size beetroots (or 8 small), I use Burpees Golden, purple Pronto and stripy Barbietola di Chioggia

8 handfuls rocket (wild or salad rocket)

125 g feta cheese, cubed

2 handfuls mint, chopped

dressing made using I part lemon juice or red wine vinegar to 2 parts extra-virgin olive oil, plus I teaspoon honey, Maldon sea salt and freshly ground black pepper

Leaving the skins on, simmer the beetroot in a pan until they are tender (20–30 minutes, depending on size). Cool them slightly and rub off the skins with your fingers. Cut them into 1–2 cm cubes and allow to cool. Put all the ingredients together in a salad bowl, pour over the dressing, toss well and sprinkle with mint leaves. Eat as soon as you've dressed it.

Celery, crayfish and potato salad
SERVES 4

Both traditionally grown celery and crayfish have a dependence on clean water, and the two go well together in this variation of Jane Grigson's salad of celery, mussels and potato. Most UK sold crayfish are produced in Norway, but British are sometimes available (see page 204 for suppliers).

600 g new potatoes

300 g celery sticks

200 g freshwater crayfish, cooked and shelled

4 tablespoons extra-virgin olive oil

juice of I lemon

leaves from 2 sprigs flatleaf parsley

black pepper

Maldon salt flakes

2 boiled eggs

Put the potatoes in a pan of water and bring to the boil. Cook until the point of a knife will slip in with just a little resistance. Remove from the heat, drain and immediately flush with cold water to prevent further cooking. Allow to cool and then cut into slices half a centimetre thick. Put in a large bowl.

Pull any tough strings from the celery stalks, and wash off any dirt. Slice them thinly, across the grain, then rinse and pat dry. Add the celery and crayfish to the bowl and toss together with the olive oil, lemon juice, parsley, some freshly ground black pepper and a pinch of Maldon salt flakes. Serve topped with half a boiled egg, and decorate with a few celery leaves.

Fresh goat's cheese and beetroot salad with red wine vinegar and walnut vinaigrette

SERVES 2

José Manuel Pizarro, chef at Tapas Brindisa in Borough Market, London, makes a wonderful goat's cheese and young beetroot salad with Monte Enebro, a new Spanish cheese made by Rafael Baez from Madrid, who signed on to an artisan cheesemaking course aged 63. Surprisingly, in the conservative world of Spanish cheese, Monte Enebro has won much acclaim and was voted best goat's cheese in Spain in 2003. You can buy Monte Enebro from Brindisa (see page 204).

1 large whole raw beetroot, or 2 small ones

1 teaspoon olive oil for roasting the beetroot

1 slice of goat's cheese (about 80 g)

1 small red onion, very thinly sliced

1 handful of mint, chervil and basil sprigs

2 tablespoons walnut halves, dry-roasted in a pan

3 tablespoons extra-virgin olive oil

2 tablespoons red wine vinegar, preferably cabernet sauvignon

freshly ground black pepper and sea salt

Preheat the oven to 200°C/Gas Mark 6. Wash the beetroot, but do not trim off the point or stalk or it will 'bleed' as it cooks. Rub with a little olive oil and cover with foil. Place in the oven for 30 minutes, then remove the foil. Roast for a further 10 to 15 minutes until tender when pierced with a knife (reduce the cooking time by 10 minutes if using small beetroot). Set aside to cool.

Cut the cheese into 2 × 1-cm sticks. Slice the beetroot and divide between two plates. Put the cheese, onion, herbs, walnuts, extra-virgin olive oil and vinegar in a bowl and mix gently, but well. Put equal amounts on to the plate with the beetroot, season with sea salt, grind over some black pepper and serve.

Prosciutto, watercress and Manchego cheese on grilled sourdough bread

SERVES 4

Chef–proprietor of his eponymous restaurant in Chicago, Charlie Trotter has the American equivalent of three Michelin stars for his epic tasting menus. This recipe shows him in a relaxed mood; those wanting the true Trotter treatment must wait until he opens his third restaurant in London.

2 tablespoons olive oil

2 teaspoons balsamic vinegar

1 clove of garlic, minced

8 slices of sourdough bread

80 g prosciutto, thinly sliced

4 slices of Manchego cheese

110 g watercress, cleaned and thick stems discarded

salt and freshly ground black pepper

Combine the olive oil, balsamic vinegar and garlic and brush on the sourdough bread. Grill the bread under a moderate heat until toasted. Arrange some of the prosciutto, cheese and watercress between two slices of bread and sprinkle with salt and freshly ground black pepper. Cut diagonally in half.

Poached asparagus with shallot and mustard vinaigrette

SERVES 4

This is Raymond Blanc's recipe cooked in his mother's kitchen in Besançon. Maman Blanc, in her eighties and undismayed that her kitchen has been invaded by her master-chef son and a group of strangers, has just leapt nimbly on to the draining board in order to retrieve an item from an upper shelf. 'In the way of mothers, she doesn't quite trust her son to provide well enough for her guests and has produced a large plate of hors d'oeuvres.' Blanc, more used to cooking in Le Manoir with a flotilla of sous chefs, retreats to view the asparagus bought that morning from Besançon market: 'white, green and a big fat purple-tipped variety that looks a bit obscene...': he is euphoric about it. 'My God, that's the best asparagus I've eaten for a long time... it has a melting texture. Often asparagus can be dry but this is juicy, buttery. It has a wonderful flavour with a tiny tinge of bitterness.'

1 tablespoon Dijon mustard
1 tablespoon white wine vinegar
sea salt
freshly ground white pepper
120 ml groundnut oil, best quality cold pressed (or any unscented oil)
1 small shallot, finely chopped
1 kg asparagus, English, medium-size, fresh local if possible

Bring a large saucepan of water (3 litres) to a galloping boil with two tablespoons of sea salt. While the water is coming to the boil, prepare the vinaigrette: in a small bowl, mix together the Dijon mustard, white wine vinegar, four tablespoons of water, a pinch of sea salt, a pinch of freshly ground white pepper, the groundnut oil and shallot.

Cut off the lower, woody parts of the asparagus stems (2–3 cm). Slide the asparagus into the fast-boiling water, taking care that all the tips are on one side of the pan, and cover with a lid to bring it back to boiling point. Remove the lid and cook for 4–5 minutes (depending on the thickness of the asparagus). Remove the asparagus with a slotted spoon and drain on a kitchen cloth. You can eat the asparagus warm or cold. (If cold, plunge the asparagus into a bowl of cold water to stop the cooking process and to retain the colour and texture.) Arrange the asparagus on a large dish and serve the vinaigrette separately.

Pecorino shortbreads with new season asparagus

SERVES 4

Thin triangles of chickpea and pecorino 'shortbread' and the season's first asparagus, dressed with a little pecorino – ewe's-milk cheese from Sardinia or Tuscany. Gram flour is available from wholefood shops and Asian grocers.

for the shortbreads

90 g gram flour, sifted

75 g mature Sardinian or Tuscan pecorino cheese, roughly grated

75 g unsalted butter, cut into cubes

½ teaspoon sea salt

pinch of freshly ground black pepper

1 tablespoon very cold water

400 g fresh asparagus, the fibrous lower end of the stalk removed

2 tablespoons freshly grated pecorino

salt and black pepper

Preheat the oven to 190°C/Gas Mark 5. Put the flour, cheese, butter and seasoning into a food processor and whizz until the mixture has a breadcrumb consistency. Add the water and whizz again. As soon as the crumbs begin to form a dough, tip them on to a board and knead together until smooth. Work quickly; the mixture should not become greasy. Wrap the dough in clingfilm and chill for 1 hour. Remove from the fridge to let it soften enough to be rolled.

Lightly flour the worktop and roll out the dough until it is about 5 mm thick. Cut it into elongated triangles, then lift onto a baking sheet lined with baking parchment or greaseproof paper. Bake for approximately 15 minutes, until the shortbreads are slightly puffed, their edges lightly brown. Lift carefully (they are very fragile) and cool on a rack.

Meanwhile bring a large pan of water to the boil. Add a pinch of salt and the asparagus. Cook for approximately 7 minutes, then lift out the asparagus and drain it on a tea towel.

Serve the shortbreads, on individual plates, with a few spears of asparagus on top scattered with a little grated pecorino. Season with salt and pepper.

Leeks vinaigrette

SERVES 4

Terence Conran's recipe uses young and slender leeks: 'They make a nice light starter or cold vegetable accompaniment. If you can't get very thin leeks you can use larger ones, split lengthways.'

8 slender leeks

2 eggs, hard-boiled, peeled and coarsely chopped

for the vinaigrette

2 tablespoons red wine vinegar

120 ml olive oil

2 tablespoons Dijon mustard

Put the leeks into a large shallow pan of lightly salted, boiling water and cook for 7–10 minutes, until tender. Make the vinaigrette. Mix all the ingredients together and season with salt and pepper. Remove the cooked leeks from the water and allow them to drain thoroughly. Arrange the leeks on a shallow dish, cover with the chopped egg, and drizzle them with lots of vinaigrette.

Eggs
Scrambled eggs with goat's cheese and green asparagus
SERVES 2

Brindisa started importing produce from small Spanish producers a decade or so ago. They now have a mail-order site based in south-east London and a shop and a tapas bar in Borough Market, London. Melt cubes of cheese at the last minute into scrambled eggs and chopped asparagus tips à la Brindisa tapas.

2 slices of sourdough bread
olive oil
8 spears of green asparagus
1 clove of garlic, chopped or crushed
4 eggs, beaten
1 thick slice of creamy goat's cheese

Brush the bread with 2 tablespoons of oil and grill on a dry pan until lightly browned on both sides. Bring a pan of water to the boil, add a pinch of sea salt and cook the asparagus for 3 minutes. Drain, then cut the spears into 3-cm pieces. Put 3 tablespoons of olive oil in a non-stick or well-seasoned heavy-bottomed pan and place over the heat. Add the garlic and cook until it just takes on a light colour. Add the eggs and stir over the heat until they thicken and scramble. When they are creamy, add the asparagus, cubes of the goat's cheese and serve with the toast. By the time it gets to the table, the cheese will have nearly melted.

Masala scrambled eggs
by Vineet Bhatia
SERVES 2

4 eggs
1 tablespoon milk
1 tablespoon coriander, finely chopped
1 tablespoon oil
1 tablespoon butter
1 medium-size red onion, finely chopped
2 green chillies, finely chopped
pinch of red chilli powder
1 tomato, finely chopped

In a bowl, beat the eggs, milk and finely chopped coriander together with some salt. In a non-stick pan heat equal quantities of oil and butter. Add the red onion and sweat until pink. Add the green chillies, a pinch of red chilli powder and the finely chopped tomato. Cook this mixture for a few minutes. Now pour in the whipped egg mixture and cook until you have a soft scrambled texture. Serve with any herb bread or flaky paratha.

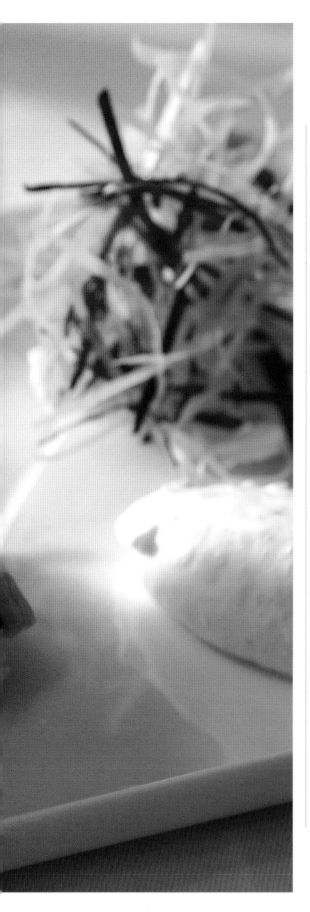

Pan-fried gull's eggs with sea trout and horseradish

SERVES 4

Gull's eggs get their status from a short season – two springtime months. It's illegal to take the eggs from wild birds, and harvesting is strictly licensed, which limits the supply and makes them a delicacy. Wild swings in weather patterns have taken their toll too. If you can find a reputable supply, however, you're in for a treat. Use Michel Roux Jr's recipe to cook them.

1 little gem lettuce
olive oil
lemon juice
4 thick slices of brioche cut into 6-cm circles
4 x 100 g slices of wild sea trout
4 tablespoons double cream
2 tablespoons horseradish relish
2 spring onions, sliced
4 gull's eggs
1 tablespoon butter

Separate the lettuce leaves, put them in a bowl and toss with a tablespoon of olive oil and a squeeze of lemon. Season with salt and pepper. Toast the brioche slices on both sides and keep warm. Pan-fry the seasoned sea trout with a drizzle of olive oil, keeping it very pink in the centre. Whisk the cream until thick, then add the horseradish. Place the brioche on four warmed plates and put a few lettuce leaves on each slice of brioche. Spoon on a generous amount of horseradish cream, sprinkle over the spring onions then place the sea trout on top. Finally, fry the eggs with the fresh butter until the whites are set and place on top of the fish.

Soups
Vegetable and herb soup
by Michael Caines

SERVES 4–5

20 g shallots, finely chopped

35 g leeks, diced into 1 cm cubes

50 g each celeriac, carrots, courgettes, tomatoes (blanched and seeded) and cabbage all diced into 1 cm cubes

150 g unsalted butter

50 ml white wine

500 ml water

500 ml chicken stock

50 g french beans

50 g peas

100 g cream

12 basil leaves, roughly chopped

5 g sorrel and 5 g chervil, roughly chopped

5 g chives, chopped

salt and freshly ground black pepper

pinch of sugar

Sweat the shallots, leeks, celeriac and carrots with 25 g of the butter and a pinch of salt for 5 minutes. Do not brown. Add the white wine and boil until reduced. Add the water and chicken stock and bring to the boil. Cook for about 10 minutes. Add the courgettes, cabbage, french beans and peas and cook for a further 5 minutes. Now add the cream and whisk in the remaining butter. Add the herbs and tomatoes. Season with salt, pepper and a pinch of sugar.

Onion soop from Court Cookery by R Smith 1725

SERVES 6–8

This soup was one of the recipes cooked by Heston Blumenthal at Hampton Court while working with the experimental archaeology team from 17th-and 18th-century cookbooks.

'Take two Quarts of strong Veal Broth, 14 large Onions, and cut them thin, and fry them tender; then burn half a Quarter of a Pound of Butter black; and toss up your fry'd Onions, and put in; then stew them Half an Hour in your Broth, and take the Yolks of eight Eggs well beaten, six Spoonfuls of Spanish Wine, and put them in a quarter of an Hour before you serve up, and keep stirring it till you send it away. Let your garnish be Bread be cut in Dice and fry'd.'

To make this recipe at home the instructions included in the original version are quite easy to follow. Halving the quantities will provide sufficient for four people. The wine measurements are given in tablespoons.

Spinach, lemon and turmeric soup

SERVES 4

Jake Tilson's wife, the ceramic artist Jennifer 'Jeff' Lee has invented a recipe for spinach and turmeric soup that turns a gloriously deep and pond-like green as it blends.

2 onions, finely chopped
55 g butter
1 kg spinach, finely chopped
juice and grated zest of 1 lemon
1 teaspoon turmeric
1.2 litres stock (chicken or ham)
4 tablespoons yogurt

Sauté the onions in the butter until transparent. Add the spinach and let it wilt, then add the lemon juice, zest, turmeric and stock. Season, cover and simmer for 30 minutes. Leave to cool, then blend in a food processor until smooth. Reheat, adding extra stock if needed. Serve with a swirl of yogurt.

Watercress and goat's cheese soup

SERVES 8

Kirsty Young's watercress and goat's cheese soup is served in chic, spotted espresso cups in non-matching colours with crab crostini (see page 58).

3 medium-size onions
2 large potatoes
olive oil
1 litre chicken or vegetable stock
4 bunches of Dorset watercress, destalked and roughly chopped
280 ml double cream
8 cubes of goat's cheese

Peel the onions and potatoes and chop into cubes. Heat the olive oil in a pan and fry the onions and potatoes for 10 minutes. Add the stock and the watercress, cook for 20 minutes and then put in a liquidiser. Stir in the cream, reheat and pour into eight small cups. Top each with a cheese cube and serve.

Tom yam kung by Joseph Budde, executive chef at the Grand Hyatt in Tokyo

SERVES 1

A particularly healthy river prawn and straw mushroom soup.

300 ml water or clear chicken broth

1 piece galangal (2–3 cm), finely sliced

2–3 kaffir lime leaves, shredded

half a lemongrass stalk, finely sliced

15–20 g straw mushrooms, cleaned and cut into quarters

80–100 g blue river prawns, peeled and de-veined

1–1½ tablespoons freshly squeezed lime juice

2–3 bird's eye chillies, crushed

1–1½ tablespoons fish sauce

a few fresh coriander leaves

a few strips of large red chilli, cored and seeded

Bring the water or broth to the boil, add the galangal, kaffir lime leaves and lemongrass and simmer for 7–10 minutes to infuse. Add the mushrooms and increase the heat a little and cook gently for 2 minutes. Add the prawns and simmer without stirring for 2–3 more minutes. Finally, add the lime juice and crushed chillies and season with fish sauce. Transfer to a warmed serving bowl and garnish with coriander leaves and chilli slices. Serve the soup very hot with a small helping of steamed jasmine rice.

Watercress soup with shellfish by Rose Prince

SERVES 4–6

Watercress and shellfish go together beautifully. Try this soup with poached oysters, langoustines or, luxuriously, with lobster. Watercress can be stringy in soup, so it is well worth taking the trouble to put it through a mouli-légumes after liquidising.

60 g butter

2 medium-size onions, chopped

1 medium-size potato, peeled and diced

600 ml whole milk

600 ml water or fresh chicken stock

2 bunches of watercress – about 300 g

8 cooked langoustines, peeled (if you buy them raw, cook for 4 minutes in simmering water seasoned with 2 cloves, 6 black peppercorns, 1 teaspoon salt and 1 tablespoon white wine vinegar)

fresh watercress leaves, to serve

Melt the butter in a pan and add the onions; cook over a low heat until soft and transparent. Add the potato with the milk and water (or stock). Cook until the potato is soft, then add the watercress. Simmer for a minute, then liquidise until very smooth; put through a mouli-légumes, discarding any 'strings'. Taste for seasoning. Serve hot, together with the peeled langoustines and some fresh watercress leaves.

Fish and Shellfish
Potted North Atlantic prawns

SERVES 4

Rose Prince's recipe for potted prawns comes from her book *The New English Kitchen*. 'I like these best when they are all together in a large, shallow dish, then carved out and put on plates with lots of toast to hand.'

400 g whole North Atlantic prawns

pinch of cayenne pepper

4 teaspoons ground mace

juice of half a lemon

60 g unsalted butter

2 sprigs of chervil, flatleaf parsley or coriander

2 chives, chopped

Shell the prawns. Mix together the prawns, spices and lemon juice, then pack them into a dish. Melt the butter gently and pour over the shellfish. Drop the herb leaves and chives on to the butter, using a spoon to submerge them. Put in the fridge to set, and eat within 3 days.

Fast spaghetti with clams
by Ferran Adrià

A surprisingly simple recipe by the notoriously experimental chef.

spaghetti (amount depends on how many you are feeding)

olive oil

1 clove of garlic, finely chopped

1 bunch parsley, chopped

stock or water, enough to cover the pasta

clams (amount will vary)

Fry the pasta in a small amount of olive oil until coloured. Add the garlic and parsley and then add the water or stock slowly, as if making risotto. When the pasta is nearly done, add the clams and cook until they are open. Drain, season and serve.

Spider crab with bronze fennel
by Rose Prince

SERVES 2

In 2005, the Marine Conservation Society launched a campaign to encourage us to eat unfamiliar fish in place of critically endangered, overfished species such as North Sea cod. The spider crab is one of these 'unfamiliar British fish', a 'neglected treasure of the British seas that comes into season in March. There is a tiny amount of meat in the body shell, but it is the white leg meat that has the real value. It breaks into beautiful clean strings when cooked. Fish merchants sell the crab ready cooked, or even with the meat freshly picked from the legs.'

To pick the white meat: use a hammer or nutcrackers to break open the legs. They are quite tough and prickly, so wear rubber gloves. Pick out the white meat and break apart the chunks. Discard any cartilage – the transparent inner bones attached to the meat. A large crab will yield about 180 g meat. Use green fennel if the bronze variety is not available.

the meat from 1 large, cooked spider crab

3 tablespoons extra-virgin olive oil

juice of 1 lemon

1 small fennel bulb, very thinly sliced

2 sprigs of soft bronze or green fennel leaves,
(or flatleaf parsley), chopped

Mix all the ingredients together and pack the mixture back into the main body shell. Serve with toast. You can change the flavour of this salad by adding red chilli, substituting the lemon for lime and the fennel for coriander.

Haddock poached in butter, with champ by Richard Corrigan

SERVES 4

Smoked haddock poached in butter and stock: 'If you poach haddock in milk,' says Corrigan, 'I find much of the fish flavour disappears... with the butter and broth that doesn't happen (and you can use the leftover broth for a potato and shellfish soup).'

200 g unsalted butter
200 ml fish stock (or vegetable)
1 very small sprig of thyme
4 pieces lightly smoked undyed haddock (or Finnan haddock), each weighing about 140 g
9 fresh raw langoustines, the shell removed (optional)
for the champ
300 g floury potatoes
120 g butter
2 tablespoons milk
sea salt
4 spring onions, thinly sliced on the diagonal
for the leftover dish (serves 2)
8 new potatoes
450 g live shellfish, cleaned (use mussels, clams or cockles)
parsley and chive leaves, chopped

First prepare the champ: boil the potatoes with their skins on until soft. Drain into a colander and rub the skins off with your fingers. Use a cloth if they are too hot. Put the cooked potatoes through a hand operated food mill (mouli-légumes) or mash them well. Whisk in the butter and the milk and add sea salt to taste. Set aside in a warm place, cover with a cloth to absorb the steam. Warm four plates.

Now for the fish: heat together the butter and stock, add the thyme and poach the haddock pieces in the stock for about 3–5 minutes until they are firm, but begin to flake apart slightly at the surface. Brush the langoustines (if using them) with a little oil and grill or cook them in a pan until they are opaque and firm.

Beat the sliced spring onion into the champ and put a spoonful on to each plate. Place a piece of fish on top, followed by three langoustines. Put about 4 tablespoons of the butter broth into a small pan and whisk over the heat until foamy, then pour a little over the fish as you serve.

To make a supper dish from the leftover broth, cook the new potatoes in the broth until just tender, then add the cleaned shellfish. Simmer until the shells have opened fully, then served scattered with the chopped fresh herbs.

Ragù di scampi with polenta integrale (wholemeal polenta)

SERVES 4

The Brandolinis, who own a vineyard in Friuli and live part of the year in a 15th-century palazzo on the Grand Canal in Venice, also run a bar/restaurant on the Grand Canal between the Rialto Bridge and the Mercato di Pesce. Naranzaria is set in an old orangerie and makes full use of the nearby fish market – stalls heaped with cuttlefish, gilt-head bream, razor clams, mazzancolle (like large prawns fished in the lagoon in Venice), monkfish, paganei (delicious in risotto) and moeche (live soft-shelled lagoon crabs). Naranzaria uses the mazzancolle in a ragù di scampe.

for the polenta

1 litre water

2 teaspoons salt

200 g imported coarse-ground cornmeal

for the ragù di scampi

4 tablespoons extra-virgin olive oil

1 clove of garlic, peeled and crushed

½ onion, finely chopped

1 stalk of celery, finely chopped

1 carrot, finely chopped

1 teaspoon fresh thyme, finely chopped

1 teaspoon fresh rosemary, finely chopped

8 very ripe cherry tomatoes, quartered lengthwise and seeds removed

350 g large shrimp, shelled and de-veined, cut into chunks

handful of fresh basil leaves

To make the polenta bring the water to a gentle boil in a heavy-bottomed pot. Add the salt, then pour the cornmeal into the pot in a steady stream, stirring continuously with a wire whisk to prevent lumps. Reduce the heat to medium. When the polenta begins to thicken, lower the heat to a minimum and stir continuously with a wooden spoon. The polenta will bubble and spit as the cornmeal thickens. Stir very frequently for 40–50 minutes. The polenta is ready when it comes away easily from the sides of the pot.

Meanwhile, make the ragù: heat the oil and gently fry the garlic clove in a medium pan for 1–2 minutes. Discard the garlic and add the chopped onion, celery, carrot, thyme and rosemary and sauté over a gentle heat until tender (about 10 minutes). Increase the heat to high, add the tomatoes and sauté for 2 minutes, stirring regularly. Add salt to taste then stir in the shrimp and sauté until it is no longer opaque, about 1 minute (no longer, or the shrimp will become chewy). Scatter in the basil leaves, spoon the ragù over the polenta and serve immediately.

Carrot butter, a sauce for fish

SERVES 4

As any Irishman will tell you, the only butter worth eating is made by Irish cows eating Irish grass in Ireland. Richard Corrigan, who is the genius behind the kitchens at Bentley's and the Lindsay House in London, is adamant on this point, noting that the Irish have been producing butter for thousands of years – 'Peat cutters on Irish bogs occasionally excavate ancient stores of butter, wrapped in animal skins or decorated wooden tubs. "Bog butter" can be anything from 100 to many thousands of years old. It has the texture of paraffin wax, but those who find it say it smells just like sweet-cream butter.' Corrigan grew up on a farm on boggy ground in Co Meath and as a boy made butter with his family.

Richard Corrigan serves this sauce with turbot, but it is just as good with brill, pollock or other fine-flavoured white fish. You can use salted butter, but do not add seasoning unless it needs it.

15 green cardamom pods

400 g unsalted butter

1 kg carrots, finely grated

vegetable stock

white wine vinegar (preferably Forum Chardonnay vinegar)

12 small carrots, peeled and left whole

4 pieces of turbot, each weighing about 230 g

4 sprigs of purslane (see page 204 for suppliers)

Crush the cardamoms and extract the seeds. Melt the butter and add the carrots and cardamom seeds. Cook at a low temperature for 3–4 minutes, then cover with stock and cook for a further 15 minutes. Take the pan from the heat and allow it to sit for at least 15 minutes so the flavours can develop and amalgamate. Set a metal sieve over a second pan and tip the contents of the first pan into it. Use the back of a wooden spoon to push as much liquid as you can through the sieve. Taste the sauce and add a drop or two of white wine vinegar to sharpen it, then add salt and pepper. Keep four shallow bowls warm. Put the peeled whole carrots in a pan of water with a large pinch of salt and cook until just tender. Set to one side, keeping them warm.

Meanwhile pan-fry the turbot for about 6–7 minutes on each side, less if the steaks are smaller. Reheat the sauce and add the leaves from the purslane sprigs. Put a piece of turbot in each bowl with three of the carrots, then ladle the sauce around.

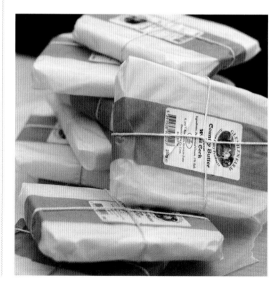

Vegetables
Orzotto con le primizie, barley 'risotto' with spring vegetables

SERVES 4

Naranzaria's Orzotto con le primizie (barley cooked like risotto with peas, asparagus and finferli – chanterelle mushrooms) is a metaphor for spring.

---

200 g pearl barley

1.25 litres chicken broth or 1 bouillon cube dissolved into 1.25 litres of simmering water

6 tablespoons extra-virgin olive oil

1 small onion, finely chopped

1 carrot, peeled and finely chopped

1 celery stalk, finely chopped

100 g green asparagus, tips set aside, stalks cut into 1 cm segments

100 g chanterelle or other wild or cultivated mushrooms, cleaned and roughly chopped

500 g fresh peas in their pods, shelled

2 tablespoons butter

90 g freshly grated Parmesan

Rinse the barley well, cover with plenty of cold water and leave to soak for at least 2 hours (and up to overnight). When the barley is ready to cook, heat the broth or bouillon to a low simmer. Warm the olive oil in a large heavy-bottomed saucepan. Add the onion, carrot and celery and sauté gently over a low flame until the vegetables are soft (about 10 minutes). Add the barley to the pan, stirring vigorously for a couple of minutes to coat it with the oil and vegetables. Add the asparagus (stalks but not tips) and enough broth to cover the mixture with about 4 cm of liquid. Stir frequently until most of the broth is absorbed. Continue adding additional broth in small amounts, stirring frequently, as it is absorbed by the barley. When the barley is cooked though still firm (about an hour), add the mushrooms, peas and asparagus tips and cook, stirring regularly, for 5 minutes. Remove the orzotto from the heat, vigorously stir in the butter and Parmesan and adjust the seasonings with salt and freshly ground black pepper. Let the orzotto rest for a couple of minutes before serving with more grated Parmesan.

Fresh harissa

SERVES 8 (plus enough to put aside in a freezer bag for 4 more servings)

Jake Tilson's cookbook, *A Tale of 12 Kitchens*, was written, illustrated and designed by himself. It's an 'eccentric, intimate scrapbook recording a gastronomic journey that has taken him from the counter-culture kitchens of a 1960s London childhood, via farmhouses in Umbria and Scotland to the food markets of Los Angeles, Tunisia and New York'. Recipes derived from this peripatetic childhood were collected by Tilson in a series of ancient exercise books that now form the bulk of his book. As you might expect, his cooking is eclectic, but a major influence is Tunisia.

Harissa originated in Tunisia and is also used in Libya and Algeria as a condiment and ingredient. Recipes swing between fiery North African and European bistro. This recipe was 'perfected on a trip to Tangiers...' For a sweeter, less fiery effect, Tilson adds Spanish smoked paprika and a large roasted piquillo pepper to the standard chilli mix. It takes a few hours, so make extra for the freezer.

200 g large, long red chillies
4 cloves of garlic, chopped
olive oil

Use rubber gloves to handle so many chillies. Slit each chilli in half lengthways. Scrape away the seeds and ridged veins inside and discard. Roughly chop the chillies and garlic. Whizz in a processor until smooth. Add a little olive oil. Divide the mix in two, and make one portion each of North African and European harissa.

to make traditional North African harissa

1 teaspoon ground coriander
1 teaspoon ground caraway seeds
1 teaspoon tomato purée
olive oil

To half the puréed chilli mix add the coriander and caraway seeds, tomato purée, 1 teaspoon of water and 1 tablespoon of olive oil.

to make European harissa

1 teaspoon ground caraway seeds
1 teaspoon ground cumin seeds
1 teaspoon ground coriander
2 teaspoons hot smoked Spanish paprika
1 large piquillo pepper, roasted, roughly chopped
1 tablespoon tomato purée
red wine vinegar
olive oil

Dry fry the ground caraway seeds and cumin seeds, add these and the ground coriander, the Spanish paprika and the piquillo pepper to the remaining half of the chilli mixture. Blend well in a processor. Transfer to a bowl and add the tomato purée, a capful of red wine vinegar and 3 tablespoons of olive oil for a piquant, sweet and smoky-tasting sauce.

Braised fennel

SERVES 12

Spring fennel, braised in oil, makes an excellent accompaniment to lamb or mutton, which tastes best with robust-flavoured vegetables. You could also try tomatoes, sweet peppers, aubergine and courgettes, pepped up with garlic.

4 fennel bulbs

10 tablespoons extra-virgin olive oil

8 tablespoons water

freshly ground black pepper

sea salt

Cut each fennel bulb into four quarters, splitting it from top to bottom. Reserve any soft, bright green, frond-like leaves to throw on to the fennel before serving. Heat the oil in a large casserole, add the fennel and allow the bulbs to 'fry' in the oil until lightly coloured. Fennel spits when cooked in oil, so be careful. Turn the fennel gently with tongs and cook the other side. Add the water. Slam on the lid and cook covered over a low heat until soft when pricked with a knife. Season with salt and pepper, add a little fresh olive oil, scatter over the fennel fronds and serve.

Watercress and potato cakes
with hot radish dressing by Rose Prince

SERVES 6

You can also make these potato cakes smaller, to eat as a snack with a bowl of the dressing for dipping.

900 g mashed potato, beaten with 60 g butter and cooled

3 eggs

1 heaped tablespoon flour

leaves from 2 bunches of watercress, roughly chopped

olive oil for frying

for the dressing

1 tablespoon grated fresh horseradish (substitute with ½–1 teaspoon of wasabi paste if you cannot find fresh horseradish)

10 French radishes, sliced

leaves from 4 radishes, chopped

3 teaspoons mustard seeds

juice of 1½ lemons

100 ml extra-virgin olive oil

Mix together the mashed potato, eggs, flour and watercress. Season to taste. Heat a generous amount of olive oil in a large non-stick frying pan; spoon a heaped tablespoon of the potato and watercress mixture into the pan and flatten with the spoon to about 2 cm thick. Fry over a low heat for 5 minutes, then flip over and fry the other side for another 5 minutes. Make the cakes in batches, keeping them warm in the oven. Meanwhile mix the dressing ingredients together and season with a pinch of sea salt. Serve the potato cakes with a spoonful of the dressing beside.

Potato torta with ricotta, Parmesan and basil by Rose Prince

SERVES 8

An Italian inspired pie, made with a paper-thin olive oil pastry and filled with mashed potato, herbs and cheeses. The eggs are optional.

for the pastry

150 g plain flour

½ teaspoon salt

1½ tablespoons extra-virgin olive oil

approximately 125 ml iced water

for the filling

4 medium-size red potatoes

1 egg, beaten

50 g fresh grated Parmesan (or substitute with 50 g grated mature cheddar)

60 g ricotta cheese, drained for an hour on a cloth

250 ml milk, heated then cooled

30 g butter

4 whole eggs

8 basil leaves

extra-virgin olive oil, for glazing

Put the flour and salt in the bowl of a table top mixer and attach the dough hook. Add the oil as it mixes, then the water, a tablespoon at a time, until the mixture forms a dough. You may not need to add all the water. Continue to mix until the dough is smooth and elastic. Wrap it in clingfilm and store in the fridge. You can make and knead the dough by hand – it will take about 15 minutes.

Meanwhile cook the potatoes in boiling water until soft. Drain and allow to cool, then rub off the skins. Pass through a food mill (mouli-légumes), then mix in the beaten egg, cheese, milk and butter.

Preheat the oven to 190°C/Gas Mark 5. Roll out the pastry into a large thin round. You will find it very elastic and pliable. Use your hands to thin and stretch it further until the pastry round is very thin and approximately 50 cm diameter. Place it over a baking sheet, spoon the filling into the centre and spread it into a round approximately 30 cm in diameter. Make four indentations, using the back of a spoon, then crack an egg into each. Throw over the basil leaves. Bring the pastry edges up and over the filling in towards the centre; stretch it if necessary. Pinch the pastry folds into the centre but leave a little hole so steam can escape as the pie cooks. Brush the surface with the oil and bake for approximately 30 minutes until golden. Can be eaten hot or cold.

Meat, Poultry and Game
Roast leg of milk-fed lamb

SERVES 2–3

The gastronomic empire started by the Harts at Hambledon Hall in Rutland has expanded into Charlotte Street in London with Fino and, latterly, Soho with Barrafina, their most recent venture, a tapas bar that dishes up exquisite plates of jamón iberico, prawns and tomato toast. Their culinary roots reside in Palma Majorca, however, where Sunday lunch, held in their house at Estellencs near Deja, comprises Serrano ham croquetas, Tumbet (a Majorcan dish of red peppers, aubergines and potatoes, see page 99) and Roast leg of milk-fed lamb. Tim Hart, father of Sam and Eddy who now run Fino and Barrafina, has trenchant theories about roasting: 'Cookery books have got roasting all wrong,' he says. 'I work with taste and feel instead of words, and principles instead of temperature. And the principles of roasting are that you must brown the outside first, then get the heat into the middle.'

oil
lamb bones, or the neck to make gravy
1 stick of celery
1 small onion, cut in half
1 carrot
1 bay leaf
2–3 sprigs of rosemary and thyme
1 leg of lamb, roughly 450–650g
225 ml red wine
root vegetables including 1 onion, 2 carrots, 2 sticks of celery, 1 leek – all roughly chopped

To make the gravy, put a little oil in a large, deep pan and sauté the bones until golden brown. Cover with cold water and simmer gently for 2 hours with the celery, onion, carrot and the bay leaf. Strain and reduce. Infuse with rosemary and thyme and season at the last minute. The reduction will achieve an intense flavour but not a thick consistency.

To cook the leg, preheat the oven to 200°C/ Gas Mark 6. Heat a little oil in a large frying pan and brown the leg on both sides. Remove the leg and keep warm. De-glaze the pan with the red wine, stirring to clean the pan, and reduce until syrupy. Add the red wine juices to the gravy. Put the leg on the root vegetables, or on a trivet over the vegetables, in a roasting pan.

Roast the leg for 15 minutes or until a skewer inserted into the thickest part is just warm. Rest the joint in a warm place for at least 20 minutes before carving the meat.

Roast loin of veal with anchoïade

SERVES 6

This recipe is by Jeremy Lee, the wonderful head chef at the Blueprint Café, 'I have 12 round the table and cook a great hunk of beef. Because I am a chef, I just turn the oven on to full heat and let it do its infernal work.'

2.4 kg topside of British veal

extra-virgin olive oil

for the anchoïade

2 cloves of garlic, peeled

2–3 small tins of good anchovies

juice of half a lemon

200–250 ml best single-estate extra-virgin olive oil

1 egg yolk

1–3 spoonfuls of very hot water

Preheat the oven to 220°C/Gas Mark 7. Rub the meat with the oil and lots of seasoning and place on a roasting dish. If very lean, roast for about 45–50 minutes (give it an hour if there's fat on it). There should be a nice puddle of brown juice in the bottom of the roasting pan to eat it with. An hour before serving, liquidise the sauce ingredients until very smooth. Carve the meat thinly and spoon over the anchoïade.

Lamb pavé with peas, shallots and mint by Rose Prince

SERVES 4-6

The pavé is a single muscle, found close to the aitchbone (hip) in the top of a leg (of lamb). The meat is very tight-grained and extremely tender, and can be cooked very quickly in a pan. It is delicious with early Jersey potatoes.

4 lamb pavés

for the braised peas

3 tablespoons unsalted butter

4 shallots, roughly chopped

8–10 tablespoons shelled peas (or frozen)

about 150 ml rich meat stock, preferably lamb*

mint

Season the lamb with black pepper and brown on all sides in a heavy-bottomed sauté pan. Cook for about 5–7 minutes – the lamb should be served pink. Remove the pavés from the pan and leave in a warm place to rest for about 10 minutes. Warm the dinner plates. Five minutes before serving, melt 1 tablespoon of the butter in the sauté pan. Add the shallots and cook for 1 minute, then add the peas, season and just cover with the stock. Bring to the boil and cook for a few minutes. Add fresh mint leaves at the end. Add the pavé to the peas to serve, or slice the meat (it is very tender so can be sliced quite thick) and divide among the plates, spooning the peas around the meat.

*Ask the butcher for 1 kg of lamb bones; roast them until browned, then put in a stock pan with 1 litre water, a celery stick, an onion and a large carrot. Simmer for at least 1½ hours until the stock is reduced and has taken on the meat flavour.

To dress chickens the Barbary way from Royal Cookery by P Lamb 1726

SERVES 4–6

This was one of the recipes cooked by Heston Blumenthal while working with the experimental archaeology team in the Hampton Court kitchens.

'When they are truss'd, beat them with a Rowling-Pin to break the Bones. Make a highseason'd Farce, and put it in the Bodies of your Chickens, then boil them in Milk with all Sorts of savoury Herbs and high Seasonings. You must take Care not to put them into the Milk till it boils; when they are enough, take them up, and lay them on the Gridiron till they are grown brown; then serve them with a Ramolade.'

To make this recipe at home: truss a chicken – roughly 1.6 kg – and then stuff the cavity with a mixture of fresh herbs (sage, parsley and thyme work well). Place the chicken into a pan of boiling milk – roughly 1.2 litres – and season with salt, pepper and some more fresh herbs, chopped. When the chicken is cooked (cooking times will vary, but roughly 1–1½ hours), remove from the milk and drain well. To give the chicken some colour, either griddle briefly on a barbecue, or use a ribbed griddle pan. The dish is served with a sauce – the 'ramolade'.

for the sauce
3 medium-size onions, sliced thinly
500 g button mushrooms, sliced thinly
50 g butter
600 ml chicken stock
1 tablespoon butter
100 g flour

Fry the onions and mushrooms in the butter until the onions are soft and translucent. Place the mushroom and onion mixture in a pan with the stock and boil until reduced by half. Mix the tablespoon of butter and the flour together to form a paste, stir in a couple of spoonfuls of the hot stock and mix well. Stir this back into the onion and mushroom stock and keep on stirring over a gentle heat until the mixture is smooth and shiny. Add salt and pepper to taste.

Thomas Keller's simple roast chicken (mon poulet roti)

SERVES 2–4

Thomas Keller, chef–owner of the French Laundry in America, explains how to roast a chicken. And, once it's done how to eat it... 'I take off the backbone and eat one of the oysters, the two succulent morsels of meat embedded here, and give the other to the person I'm cooking with. But I take the chicken butt for myself. I could never understand why my brothers always fought over that triangular tip – until one day I got the crispy, juicy fat myself. These are the cook's rewards.'

1 x 1–1.3 kg organic chicken

2 teaspoons minced thyme (optional)

unsalted butter

Dijon mustard

Preheat the oven to 230°C/Gas Mark 8. Rinse the chicken, then dry it very well with paper towels, inside and out. Salt and pepper the cavity then truss the bird with twine. Now, salt the chicken – I like to rain the salt (about 1 tablespoon) over the bird. Season to taste with pepper. Place the chicken in a roasting pan and put in the oven. Roast it until it's done (50–60 minutes). Remove from the oven and add the thyme to the pan. Baste the chicken with the juices and thyme and let it rest for 15 minutes on a carving board. Remove the twine. Separate the middle wing joint and eat that immediately. Remove the legs and thighs. Cut the breast down the middle and serve it on the bone, with one wing joint still attached to each. Slather the meat with fresh butter. Serve with mustard on the side and, if you wish, a simple green salad.

Bread sauce to go with roast chicken

Fergus Henderson's bread sauce makes an excellent addition to Keller's perfect chicken.

yesterday's good white bread, crusts removed and turned into breadcrumbs

milk

1 onion, peeled, left whole and studded with a dozen cloves

knob of butter

Take an educated guess at how much milk you will need to soak your breadcrumbs (roughly 100 g crumbs to 600 ml of milk). Pour the milk into a pan, add the clove-studded onion and gently heat, catching the milk before it boils. Add the crumbs to the hot milk and set aside to infuse. When the chicken is ready, remove the onion from the sauce and return the pan to the stove and stir. Add the butter and season to taste. When the sauce is thoroughly warmed through and the butter melted, it's ready to serve.

Duck confit

SERVES 4

Simon Hopkinson's recipe for duck confit is a 'real favourite. I do it with fried potatoes, parsley and garlic, crisp and golden and cooked in fat, a dish to smell.' It's part of his plan to reintroduce the nation to plain, good cooking – real cooking. 'I feel I have a few very definite things to say about the practice of good cookery in this country... to remind us all of good things neglected, forgotten or undervalued... the woodcock, the vanished fish markets of our coastal towns and the mums who once cooked from the land and not from the deep freeze...'

Confit is always best made from the legs of a bird. Duck or goose fat can be purchased in jars or tins from good food shops.

4 tablespoons good-quality salt (Maldon or French sel gris, if you can get it)

4 teaspoons sugar

6–7 sprigs of fresh thyme

2 bay leaves

10 black peppercorns

a generous grating of nutmeg

4 fatty duck legs

about 570–700 ml of duck or goose fat, depending on the size of your cooking pot

6–8 cloves of garlic, unpeeled and bruised

Grind the first six ingredients into a fine powder. Pour half of it into a shallow dish and place the duck legs flesh-side down on this. Sprinkle over the rest of the spice mix, cover with clingfilm and put in the fridge, or a cool place, for 18–24 hours, turning the legs over once halfway through the process.

Preheat the oven to 130°C/Gas Mark 1. Melt the fat in a solid cast-iron pot over a low heat. Rinse the duck legs under running water and slide them into the fat together with the garlic. Bring the fat up to a gentle simmer and then place in the oven. Cook for about 2 hours, or until a metal skewer shows so little resistance to the meat that it might almost not be there.

Allow to cool and store in a suitable pot or simply the dish you cooked the confit in, but do make sure that the meat is completely covered by fat. Keep in the fridge for at least 3–4 weeks, attempting (I usually fail miserably) not to eat it before then, as it benefits hugely from this storage period. You may, of course, leave it longer than this – anything up to 4 months. Serve with fried potatoes.

Puddings
Hinds Head quaking pudding
by Heston Blumenthal

SERVES 4

Heston Blumenthal, more usually to be found in his gastronomic lab at Bray, has an alternate existence working with the experimental archaeology team based at Hampton Court. The historians are attempting not only to show how the cavernous Tudor kitchens would have looked in the days when they were catering for the court of Henry VIII but also to decipher surviving cookbooks used to prepare dishes from the Tudor, Stuart and Georgian periods. They were struck by the similarities between Heston's 21st-century chemical experiments with techniques and flavours and the methods used by 16th-century cooks, hence his presence in the kitchens while they try to reproduce a banquet served during the reign of George II – Onion soop (see page 20), lobster loaves, Chicken the Barbary way (see page 43), Scotch collops and bacon sauce and Quaking pudding. Quaking pudding is a sort of 18th-century cross between a crème caramel and blancmange served piping hot. 'They look a bit like silicone implants,' noted Blumenthal.

4 egg yolks
1 whole egg
65 g sugar
100 ml whole milk
400 ml whipping cream
a pinch of cinnamon
a pinch of nutmeg

Whisk the eggs and sugar together in a bowl. Put the milk and cream into a saucepan and bring to the boil. When it has boiled, pour the milk and cream into the egg and sugar mixture, and add the cinnamon and nutmeg. Grease and flour four 150 ml moulds. Pour the mixture into the moulds and cook in a bain-marie until the inside temperature of the puddings reaches 90°C (about an hour in an oven at 100°C/Gas Mark ½; use a thermometer). Allow to cool for 10 minutes and serve.

Clotted cream and cinnamon ice-cream

SERVES 4–6

Clotted cream makes a wonderfully rich addition to a basic ice-cream mixture. The inclusion of a stick of cinnamon makes Paul Gaylor's ice-cream a terrifically good accompaniment to apple-based deserts.

6 egg yolks

125 g caster sugar

500 ml full-cream milk

1 vanilla pod, split

1 stick of cinnamon

100 g clotted cream

Whisk the egg yolks with a third of the sugar until it becomes creamy and thick in texture. Bring the milk with the remaining sugar, vanilla pod and cinnamon stick to the boil, leave to cool slightly, then quickly pour over the beaten egg mixture, whisking continually. Strain the mixture through a strainer and return to the pan over a moderate heat, keeping stirring until the custard coats the back of a spoon. Allow the mixture to cool, and then churn for 15–20 minutes in an ice-cream maker, before adding the clotted cream. Churn until the mixture is thick and creamy. Place in the freezer until required. If you don't have an ice-cream maker, simply whisk the clotted cream into the warm custard, then cool completely and place in a plastic tub in the freezer. Check every half an hour or so and beat the ice-cream until it becomes thick and creamy in texture.

Cranberry and zinfandel jelly

SERVES 6

Choose a fruity red Californian zinfandel wine for this clean-flavoured jelly to eat after a big dinner.

675 g cranberries

240 g caster sugar

100 ml zinfandel

300 ml water

2 sachets (11 g each) powdered gelatine

for decoration: a few extra cranberries, one egg white and caster sugar

Put the fruit, sugar, wine and water into a pan and bring to the boil. Simmer for 5 minutes then remove from the heat. Strain through a sieve. Put the liquid in a clean pan and sprinkle the gelatine over the surface. Whisk to dissolve completely. Pour into individual glasses and allow to set in the fridge. Decorate the jellies before serving with cranberries that have been dipped in egg white then rolled in sugar.

Pancakes

SERVES 4

Amy Willcock's Aga recipe for pancakes uses bicarbonate of soda – 'Then they'll rise like those wonderful small, thick American ones. They make a brilliant pudding, layered with fruit and drenched in syrup.'

240 g plain flour
1 tablespoon caster sugar
1 teaspoon baking powder
4 teaspoons bicarbonate of soda
a pinch of salt
1 large egg
240 ml buttermilk
30 ml sunflower oil
1 teaspoon vanilla extract
a little extra oil, for greasing simmering plate
honey or maple syrup and butter, to serve

Put all the main ingredients into a bowl and mix really well with a whisk so there are no lumps. Place a round piece of Bake-O-Glide on the simmering plate and grease with a little oil. Cooking the pancakes in batches, drop a tablespoon of the pancake mix on to the surface and cook until it starts to bubble. Flip the pancake over and cook until puffed up. Serve with honey or maple syrup and butter. For conventional cooking, heat a little oil in a frying-pan on a medium heat, drop a tablespoon of the batter in and cook as above.

Honeycomb cream with hazelnut meringue by Rose Prince

SERVES 6

Whipped cream, chunks of honeycomb and nutty meringue. Serve in glasses or a pretty glass bowl.

2 egg whites
120 g golden icing sugar, sifted
90 g chopped hazelnuts
400 ml double cream
120 g cut honeycomb

Preheat the oven to 150°C/Gas Mark 2 and line two baking sheets with baking parchment. Put the egg whites and icing sugar in a large bowl and beat with an electric whisk until stiff peaks of white foam are formed. This will take about 9 minutes, so a table-top food mixer is best, although you can use a handheld mixer. Fold the nuts into the meringue. Drop small dessertspoonfuls of the mixture on to the baking parchment, 5 cm apart. You should fit approximately nine on each sheet. Bake for 30 minutes until very pale brown and slightly cracked. Allow the meringues to cool on the trays then lift them off the baking parchment. Whip the cream, cut the honeycomb into rough chunks and fold together roughly. Serve spooned over the meringue.

Blueberries with lime sugar

SERVES 4

Anthony Bourdain's recipe for blueberries with lime is surprising in that Bourdain, the author of *Kitchen Confidential*, the American culinary exposé that reads like a Tarantino script, is famously keen on 'everything to do with blood, guts and gore'. It tastes stunning though and is simplicity itself, underlining Bourdain's trenchant, and entirely sensible, advice on cooking for others: 'Don't do anything complicated that requires you stand over it in front of people who haven't seen you naked.'

3 tablespoons sugar
juice of 2 limes
850 g blueberries
1 sprig of mint, leaves cut into a chiffonnade (ultra-thin slice)
110 ml crème fraîche (or sour cream)
for the lime-zest confit
(you can make this in advance and store in an airtight container in the fridge)
2 limes
225 ml water
110 g sugar

In a large bowl, combine the sugar and lime juice and stir to dissolve the sugar. Add the blueberries and toss well. To make the confit, remove the peel from the limes with a paring knife. Cut away the white pith from the peel and cut the remaining zest into thin strips. (You can also use a canneleur, a tool that makes nice strips of zest.) Combine the water and sugar in a small pot and bring to the boil. Add the strips of lime zest and reduce to a simmer.

Loosely cover the pot and let the liquid cook until it is reduced by half. Remove from the heat and allow to cool completely. Add the mint and confit to the blueberries and toss well again. Serve with the crème fraîche on the side.

Knickerbocker glory

SERVES 1

The quintessential English sundae imported from America. Frozen raspberries work just as well as fresh. Serve in tall glasses with long spoons.

in a sundae glass layer the following
chocolate syrup
a scoop of vanilla ice-cream
crushed raspberries
a scoop of mango ice-cream
crushed pineapple
a scoop of dark chocolate ice-cream
finally
top with whipped cream and a cherry

Apple snow

SERVES 4

A useful way of using up the end of last season's apples. From *The New English Kitchen* by Rose Prince.

---

2 egg whites

120 g golden caster sugar

375 ml unsweetened apple sauce, puréed

a pinch of cinnamon

4 teaspoons golden muscovado sugar

Whisk the egg whites until stiff and fold in the caster sugar. Whisk again until shiny and smooth. Mix the apple with the cinnamon and fold into the egg-white mixture. Divide the mixture among glasses or bowls and sprinkle muscovado sugar on top of each.

Crème brûlée

SERVES 12

This is the crème brûlée recipe devised by David Fransonet, the Hennessy chef at the family's Chateau Bagnolet on the banks of the Charente. The combination of cream and cognac (which you just pour over the brûlée at the last minute) is stupendous and has the advantage of not cooking the alcohol.

---

13 egg yolks

250 g caster sugar

1 litre milk

250 ml single cream

3 dessertspoons strong coffee

brown sugar for sprinkling

12 measures of Hennessy VS

Make the day before. Preheat the oven to 110 °C/ Gas Mark 2. Whisk the egg yolks and sugar together in a bowl. Heat the milk, cream and coffee to boiling point and stir into the egg and sugar mixture. Pour into individual ramekins and bake in a bain-marie in the oven for an hour. Cool, then leave to set in the fridge for 24 hours. To serve, sprinkle each ramekin with brown sugar and either caramelise with a blowtorch or brown under a hot grill until bubbling. Pour a measure of Hennessy over each crème brûlée and serve immediately.

Summer

(JUNE, JULY, AUGUST)

'Summer has set in with its usual severity'

Samuel Taylor Coleridge (1772–1834)

Summer uniform bursting at the seams, the lack of cheap flights and children fraught with exam tension does indeed invoke a feeling of severity in even the best-intentioned mother. Your spouse may be out playing cricket, but you are quite likely spending the summer wondering how to feed an influx of teenagers on 'study leave' who are supposed to be revising for their GCSEs but are in fact in your kitchen looking for sustenance. Their schools have apparently washed their hands of them until speech day and the imminent publication of league tables, and you are left with the job of nurturing a free-range family who must come and go as they please, no longer curfewed by darkness and, due to an excess of fresh air, hungry at all hours. Summery salads and cold repasts, soups hot and cold and a freezer full of cooling puds is the answer. You can leave them out for consumption while you escape to work. The only other things needed for a stress-free culinary summer are a cupboardful of barbecue staples and a couple of posh main courses to impress summer visitors. Rose Prince, Jamie Oliver, Pippa Small, Fergus Henderson and Sophie Grigson show you how.

Breakfasts
Bircher muesli

200 g rolled oats

juice of half a lemon

110 ml water

2 sour green apples, such as Granny Smith

700 ml plain yogurt

6 tablespoons honey

fresh or poached fruit, to serve

4 tablespoons roasted hazelnuts, skinned and crushed, to serve

Mix the oats, lemon juice and water together in a bowl. Cover and soak overnight. In the morning, grate the apples, with their skin on, and mix with the soaked oats, yogurt and honey. To serve, divide the muesli between four bowls, top with your fruit selection and sprinkle with the hazelnuts.

Mango lassi
MAKES 2 GLASSES

The recipe is from Lahore, the city restaurant frequented by Helen Mirren and Imran Khan.

2 parts whole milk

1 part whole yogurt

4 generous slices of ripe mango

2 teaspoons sugar

ice – about four cubes per helping

Put all the ingredients into a blender and whizz until foamy. If the lassi is very thick, add water. Pour into glasses and refrigerate before serving.

Brioche by Amy Willcock
MAKES ONE LOAF

40 g fresh yeast

50 ml warm milk

1 kg plain flour

100 g unrefined golden caster sugar

700 ml water

12–15 eggs

20 g salt

700 g unsalted butter, softened

for the glaze

1 egg yolk, beaten with 1 tablespoon milk

Crumble the yeast into the milk and mix until smooth. Put the flour and sugar into the bowl of an electric mixer with the dough hook attached and start the mixer on slow. Pour in the yeast and milk and water, then add the eggs one at a time. Add the salt and butter and knead well. It will appear very sloppy but persevere. When the dough comes away from the sides of the bowl it is ready. Put the dough in a lightly greased bowl and leave it in a warm place for 1–2 hours or until it has doubled in size; then knock back the dough and return it to the bowl. Chill in the fridge for a few hours. Turn out the dough and shape it into a ball or plait or transfer to a tin. Leave to rise again until it has doubled in size, then glaze the top with the egg yolk mix. Preheat the oven to 200°C/Gas Mark 6 and bake for 40–45 minutes or until it is golden and sounds hollow when tapped. If you are using a tin, unmould and cool on a wire rack. If you have an Aga, place on a grid shelf on the third set of runners in the roasting oven and bake as above.

Starters and Al Fresco Lunches
Szechuan green beans

SERVES 4 AS A FIRST COURSE

Sophie Grigson lives in bucolic splendour
in Oxfordshire, in a cottage surrounded by
fruit trees, pots of herbs and raised stone veg
beds – the Chiltern hills rolling away into
the distance. She cooked this delicious mix
of shrimps and beans for an al fresco lunch
that, owing to sheets of rain, took place inside.
Dried shrimps and Szechuan pepper can be
found in Chinese food shops.

2 tablespoons dried shrimps

450 g French beans, topped and tailed

sunflower or vegetable oil for deep-frying

2 cloves of garlic, peeled and thinly sliced

4 teaspoons Szechuan peppercorns or black
peppercorns, coarsely crushed

2.5 cm piece of fresh ginger, peeled and cut into
matchsticks

4 teaspoons salt

1 tablespoon sugar

1 tablespoon dark soy sauce

2 teaspoons rice vinegar or white wine vinegar

1 tablespoon sesame oil

Cover the shrimps generously with boiling water
and soak for 20 minutes. Drain and reserve the
liquid. Chop the shrimps finely. Heat a panful of oil
to 190°C and deep fry the beans for 5 minutes until
tender and patched with brown. Drain on kitchen
paper. In a wok or large high-sided frying pan heat
a tablespoon of oil until it smokes. Add the garlic,
pepper and ginger, and stir-fry for a few seconds.
Then add the shrimps and stir-fry for 30 seconds.
Add the salt, sugar, soy sauce and 5 tablespoons of
the shrimp water. Finally, add the green beans. Toss
in the sauce to coat well, then cover and, keeping
the heat high, cook until virtually all the liquid has
been absorbed. Check after 1 minute – the sauce
should have caramelised and the beans should
be several shades darker, even verging on black.
Toss and, if necessary, cover again for a further 30
seconds or so to finish cooking. Remove from the
heat and mix with the rice vinegar and sesame oil.
Serve hot or, better still, at room temperature.

Tomato and ewe's-milk cheese timbales

MAKES 4

Little moulds of fresh cheese, layered with tomatoes, peppers, aubergines and herbs, to eat as a starter or small supper dish.

softened butter

1 aubergine, baked whole in the oven until soft

4 strips of roasted, peeled peppers

90 g sunblush tomatoes, drained of oil

2 eggs

240 g Brousse cheese, a Corsican fromage frais (you can use fresh goat's cheese or cream cheese as an alternative)

4 sprigs of basil, torn into shreds

Preheat the oven to 190°C/Gas Mark 5. Butter four timbale moulds or ceramic ramekins. Scoop the flesh from the aubergine, chop finely with the peppers and tomatoes, and set aside. Separate the eggs. Beat the cheese with the egg yolks and season with salt and freshly ground black pepper. Whisk the egg whites and fold them into the cheese mixture. To assemble the timbales, spoon a layer of cheese mixture into each mould, followed by a few basil leaves and a thin layer of the tomato, pepper and aubergine mixture. Follow this with another layer of cheese and repeat until the moulds are full. (If you have any of the tomato mixture left, add a little olive oil to it and use later as a sauce.) Put the moulds in a roasting pan in 2 cm of boiling hot water. Bake for 15 minutes until set. Unmould on to plates and serve with rocket salad.

Crab crostini

SERVES 8

Kirsty Young's recipe for crab crostini. It makes an excellent starter with her watercress soup (see page 22).

225 g white Dorset crabmeat

juice of 1 lemon

2 thinly diced red chillies

1 ciabatta loaf cut into thin slices, roughly 16 pieces

olive oil

Mix the crabmeat, lemon juice and chillies together and allow to sit in the fridge for up to 24 hours. On the day, preheat the oven to 180°C/Gas Mark 4. Drizzle the slices of ciabatta with olive oil. Place on a baking tray and bake for 5–10 minutes. Remove from oven and spread each slice with the crab mixture. Serve on a large plate with cold white wine.

Tomato and ricotta tarts

MAKES 8 INDIVIDUAL TARTS

I courgette, sliced into rounds

360 g ready-made puff pastry

240 g ricotta

8 tablespoons sunblush tomatoes, drained of oil

extra-virgin olive oil

8 small sprigs of fresh oregano

Preheat the oven to 230°C/Gas Mark 8. Lay the courgette slices in a hot, dry pan on the stove and brown on each side. Roll the pastry on a floured board to 2 cm thickness. Use a coffee saucer as a template to cut eight rounds, and place them on two oiled baking trays. Prick each several times to prevent them rising too far. Divide the ricotta, courgette and tomatoes between the tarts, placing a spoonful of each on each one. Spoon about a tablespoon of oil on each tart, season, then bake for 10–15 minutes, until the pastry is golden and crisp. Scatter on the oregano leaves, letting them wilt while the tarts are hot, and serve.

Pea mousse, peas, pea shoots, ricotta cheese and Parma ham

SERVES 4

Tom Aikens, the James Dean of the culinary world, is a dangerously romantic presence in the kitchen – you just don't know what he is going to do next… His food, on the other hand, is consistently excellent: light, brilliantly coloured and full of flavour. His recipe for pea mousse is complicated but worth the effort.

700 g fresh peas

3 gelatine leaves, soaked

juice of 2 lemons

sugar

150 g whipped cream

12 leaves fresh mint, cut finely

100 g ricotta cheese

4 slices Parma ham

2 punnets fresh pea shoots

olive oil

Cook the peas in boiling water until tender and then, reserving some of the liquid, refresh 200 g of them in iced water. Place the rest in a blender with the gelatine and purée with a little of the cooking water, juice of a lemon, sugar to taste and some salt. Pass through a fine sieve and place over a bowl of ice to cool. When the mixture is almost set, gently add the whipped cream and mint. Put in the fridge to set. Crush the rest of the peas with a fork and blend in the ricotta with a little more lemon juice, salt, pepper and 100 ml olive oil. Spoon the mousse into quenelle shapes, plating with some of the ricotta-and-pea mix. Place the ham on top. Dress the shoots in a little olive oil, lemon juice, salt and pepper and arrange on top of the ham.

Peperonata bruschetta
with cured ham
SERVES 6

Peperonata is brilliantly multi-functional –
you can serve it hot, warm or at room
temperature, as part of a mixed hors d'oeuvre
or as a vegetable side dish with meat, poultry
or fish. Sophie Grigson says, 'I like it tossed
into pasta with a little grated Parmesan,
and I've even had it spread on a pizza with
mozzarella, anchovies and black olives.' Here
it is spread on garlicky bruschetta with a twist
of cured ham.

1 onion, sliced
4 tablespoons extra-virgin olive oil
4 red peppers, de-seeded, de-stemmed and cut into long strips
1 red chilli, de-seeded and chopped
2 cloves of garlic, crushed
450 g tomatoes, skinned and roughly chopped
1 tablespoon tomato purée
1 teaspoon sugar (unless your tomatoes are exceptionally good)
a good pinch of aniseed (optional)
to serve
slices of griddled bread; halved cloves of garlic; a few slices of cured ham, such as jamón Serrano, or Parma ham, cut into strips; sprigs of basil

Sauté the onion in the olive oil until lightly
browned. Add the peppers, chilli and garlic and
cook for a further couple of minutes. Cover the pan
and let them cook down gently in their own juices
for 10 minutes. Now add the remaining ingredients,
bring to the boil, then simmer gently for half an
hour, uncovered, stirring occasionally. Taste and
adjust the seasoning and leave to cool. Shortly
before serving griddle the bread, and rub one side
of each slice with the cut side of a clove of garlic.
Top with peperonata, a curl of ham and a sprig
of basil.

Herb tart
SERVES 4

350 g shortcrust pastry
egg yolk for brushing pastry
360 g Burland Green organic cheese (or brie), rinds removed, cut into chunks
500 ml single cream
3 large eggs
1 teaspoon brown sugar
1 small clove of garlic, chopped
2 handfuls finely chopped tarragon, parsley and fennel leaf

Grease a 28 cm flan dish with a removable base.
Line with the pastry, bake blind for 10 minutes.
Brush with egg yolk and return to the oven for
5 minutes. Place the diced cheese in the flan base.
Mix together all the remaining ingredients and pour
over the cheese. Cook at 180°C/Gas Mark 4 for
30 minutes. Rest for 20 minutes before serving. For
a change, use either of these combinations of herbs:
hyssop, dill and a small amount of lovage (this has
a very strong flavour); chives, marjoram and fennel
leaf. Serve with a sharp salad.

Tortilla with courgette, mint and Spanish ham

SERVES 4

This recipe was made by Sam and Sam Clark for an Andalucian picnic. 'The choice of place to eat had been the subject of heated discussion; [a local farmer] had shown us an enchanting meadow with a shady stream. We thought we had found the ideal place, until we were told that this was the very spot where a family feud had led to his father accidentally cutting off his mother-in-law's head with a scythe.'

9 tablespoons olive oil

1 medium-size onion, diced small

4 medium-size courgettes, sliced into thin rounds

1 tablespoon fresh mint, chopped

4 large organic eggs

100 g jamón (cured Spanish ham), preferably good quality such as pata negra, thinly sliced

Place a medium saucepan over a medium heat and add 4 tablespoons of the olive oil. When hot, add the onion and a pinch of salt and stir well. While the onion is cooking put the sliced courgettes into a colander and sprinkle over a teaspoon of fine sea salt, toss well and leave to drain for 10–15 minutes. As the onion colours, stir occasionally. Now add half the mint and all the courgettes (dry slightly with a cloth first), and mix well with the onion. Cook for 10–15 minutes, stirring until the courgettes are soft. Add the remaining mint, taste for seasoning, remove from the heat, drain off any excess oil and set aside. Break the eggs into a bowl and whisk. Add the courgette mix, stirring well with the egg.

Check for seasoning (it may only need a grind of black pepper). Place a frying pan over a high heat and add 3 tablespoons of the olive oil. When hot, gently pour in the egg mixture. Turn down the heat and fry for 3–5 minutes until the underside is golden brown. Then take a plate of a similar size and rest it over the pan. With both hands and two kitchen cloths, carefully invert the tortilla on to the plate. The uncooked side will still be fairly runny so watch out. Turn the heat to high again, add the last 2 tablespoons of olive oil to the pan and slide the tortilla back into the pan runny side down, and tuck in the edges. Cook for another 3 minutes. Both sides should now be golden brown; if not it requires a little more cooking. The tortilla will be cooked if it feels solid; if not continue to cook until it is firm. Remove from the heat and slide on to a plate. Allow to cool before serving in wedges with the ham slices on top.

Soups
Pappa al pomodoro

SERVES 4

Jamie Oliver's pappa al pomodoro is a filling Tuscan bread and tomato soup, on the menu at Fifteen. 'This recipe is so simple and delicious, it's unbelievable,' Oliver enthuses. 'Remember, though, you only get out of it what you put in. Don't even think of trying it with unripe tomatoes or poor-quality oil.'

good quality extra-virgin olive oil, the best you can get

4 cloves of fresh garlic, peeled

4 red chillies, de-seeded and chopped

a bunch of basil (including stalks)

2 x 400 g cans of good quality tomatoes

3 double handfuls (your hands cupped together) ripe cherry tomatoes

2 handfuls stale ciabatta bread, crusts removed, ripped into thumb-size pieces

Preheat the oven to 170°C/Gas Mark 3. Heat a saucepan and add a splash of olive oil. Finely slice 2 cloves of garlic, and add, with the chillies, to the oil. When the garlic is golden brown, throw in a sprig of basil, stir briefly and then add the canned tomatoes. Cook very gently until reduced by half. Put two-thirds of the cherry tomatoes in a roasting tray with the rest of the garlic and another sprig of basil. Season, drizzle with olive oil and roast in the oven for half an hour or so, or until the skins are broken and lovely sticky juices have begun to seep out. Blanch the rest of the tomatoes for 10 seconds in boiling water, then spoon out into ice-cold water – the skins should peel off easily. Put to one side. Meanwhile pour just enough of the boiling water on the bread to moisten it. Pour the roast tomatoes into a sieve over the pan with the cooked, canned tomatoes in it and gently push down on them so the juices drain into the pan beneath. The pips and skin can be discarded. Add the peeled tomatoes and bring gently back to the boil. Turn the heat off, season and fold in the bread with lots of torn basil leaves and more olive oil. The soup shouldn't be too runny, but if it's very thick, add more of the tomato water. Check the seasoning, and serve with more olive oil over the top.

Salmorejo (Cold tomato and pepper soup)

SERVES 4

450 g breadcrumbs, moistened with water and well drained

250 ml olive oil

250 g ripe tomatoes, skinned, de-seeded and coarsely chopped

250 g green peppers, de-seeded and finely chopped

3 cloves of garlic, peeled

1 teaspoon sherry vinegar

for the garnish

1 tablespoon olive oil

1 slice of bread, cubed

1 hard-boiled egg, chopped

25 g chopped Serrano or dry-cured ham

Place all the soup ingredients in a food processor and blend until smooth. Place in a bowl and refrigerate until ready to serve – it should be much thicker than a gazpacho. Just before serving, heat the oil in a pan, and fry the bread until crisp and brown. Garnish with the bread, egg and ham.

Bouillabaisse

SERVES 8

Alice Thomas Ellis got it right when she said that to make a successful bouillabaisse, 'you need the hot sun of Provence, the exuberant and voluble waiter, the *Marseillais*, bubbling with enthusiasm over his famous local dish'. Failing that you need a good fishmonger and an accessible recipe. This one, devised by Franck Leibeiz, head chef at the Cheyne Walk Brasserie in London, is the one to follow.

3 onions, chopped

2–3 tablespoons olive oil

I whole garlic head, peeled and chopped

5 tomatoes, diced

I teaspoon saffron

3 sticks dried fennel

4 potatoes, cut into I cm slices

fish for the stock (leave whole)

500 g conger eel

500 g velvet swimming crab

500 g scorpion fish

500 g weever fish

fish that will be served (cut into fillets)

100 g cuttlefish

100 g sea bream

100 g grouper

100 g gurnard

100 g John Dory

To make the stock: fry the onions in the oil and add the garlic and diced tomatoes. Then add all the fish for the stock (your fishmonger should have removed the venomous spines of the scorpion and weever fish). Pour on enough water to reach about I cm above the fish and vegetables. Add the saffron and dried fennel and simmer for half an hour. Add salt and pepper to taste.

To make the bouillabaisse: after half an hour, remove the cooked fish from the stock, add the cut potato and simmer in the stock for a further 5 minutes. Start to add the uncooked pieces of fish to the stock one at a time, according to the cooking times of each fish: cuttlefish, 15 minutes; sea bream, 12 minutes; grouper, 12 minutes; gurnard, 7 minutes; John Dory, 7 minutes.

for the rouille

3 baking potatoes

3 egg yolks

½ teaspoon saffron

2 large cloves of garlic, crushed

250 ml olive oil

500 ml vegetable oil

to serve

6–8 cloves of garlic, peeled

8 toast slices

8 dessertspoons Gruyère cheese, grated

8 lemon wedges

I bunch of parsley, chopped

Boil the potatoes in their skins until cooked. Peel the cooked potato, mash and allow to cool. Lightly mix in the egg yolks, saffron and garlic, and start to drizzle in the oils slowly (as you would for making mayonnaise).

Serve the bouillabaisse in large warmed soup bowls. Rub the pieces of toast with the garlic cloves, spread each piece with a good dollop of rouille, sprinkle with the Gruyère cheese and chopped parsley and squeeze on a dash of lemon. Place one piece of toast in the bottom of each soup bowl and spoon the soup, including the fish, over the toast. Serve.

Potage de petits pois

SERVES 4

Father of six and a Michelin-starred chef, John Burton Race believes there is nothing children shouldn't eat. This summery soup formed part of a family weekend lunch that included asparagus, confit of duck and Raspberry and pine kernel tart (see page 111).

2 kg fresh peas in the pod
50 g unsalted butter
1 shallot, peeled and chopped
1 clove of garlic, peeled and chopped
1 sprig of fresh thyme
1 bay leaf
450 ml chicken stock
450 ml milk
juice of half a lemon
for the garnish
1 tablespoon malt vinegar
12 quail's eggs
1 dessertspoon white truffle oil (optional)
25 g pea shoots or pods cooked in unsalted butter
4 sprigs of fresh chervil

First shell the peas, then melt the butter in a saucepan, add the shallot and garlic and sweat these in the pan to soften a little. Stir in the thyme, bay leaf and peas, then pour in the chicken stock and milk. Bring the liquid to the boil as quickly as possible and simmer for 20 minutes. Pour the mixture into a liquidiser and blend until smooth. Season and add lemon juice to taste. Strain the soup into another saucepan, bring to the boil and leave to simmer.

For the garnish, fill a saucepan with 1 litre of water, add the vinegar and bring to the boil. With the point of a small sharp knife, make a hole in the tip of a quail's egg and carefully break the egg into the water. Repeat the process as quickly as possible with the other eggs, keeping the water always just below the boil. As soon as the eggs are set but the yolks are still soft (which takes about 2 minutes), remove the eggs using a slotted spoon. Place them straight into a bowl of iced water to refresh and prevent them cooking further. To serve, place three poached quails eggs in the bottom of each warmed-up soup bowl. Bring the soup back up to the boil, add the truffle oil (if using) and blend the soup with a hand blender until light and frothy. Ladle the soup over the eggs, garnish with shoots or pods and the chervil, and serve at once.

Salads
Caesar salad

SERVES 4–6

This is the original recipe, served by Caesar Cardini in Tijuana for an unexpected coachload of revellers – it has no anchovies, but they can be chopped finely and added with the oil. The Romaine leaves were originally left whole so the salad could be eaten with fingers, but tear them up if you wish.

2 cloves of garlic, crushed

175 ml olive oil

6 tablespoons cubed white bread – use good French-style sourdough

leaves from two heads of Romaine lettuce, or four baby Cos, washed and chilled

2 eggs, boiled in the shell for 1 minute

juice of 2 lemons

8 drops of Worcestershire sauce

6 tablespoons freshly grated Parmesan cheese

Put the garlic in the olive oil and leave for 1 hour or more to infuse. Preheat the oven to 200°C/Gas Mark 6. Brush the bread with some of the oil and bake until golden. Put the leaves in a big bowl, and break the eggs over them. Toss the salad slowly, then add the lemon juice, the Worcestershire sauce and seasoning. Toss the salad again. Add the bread and cheese, toss one more time and serve.

Broad bean salad

SERVES 4

Although most often associated with flower arranging, Jane Packer has another secret life in her small cottage kitchen in Suffolk. She can often be found there cooking the results of foraging trips to local farmers' markets and delis.

125 g smoked lardons or pancetta

2 cloves of garlic, finely chopped

250–350 g young broad beans, shelled

250–350 g young asparagus spears

mixed salad leaves, such as frisée, lamb's lettuce and rocket

olive oil

tarragon vinegar

sprig of coriander, to serve

Preheat a heavy-based frying pan until hot. Lightly sauté the lardons and garlic in a little oil. Gently cook the broad beans and asparagus in a little boiling salted water for just a few minutes. Dress the salad leaves with a little olive oil and tarragon vinegar. Combine all the ingredients and serve with a sprig of coriander.

Grilled figs with Bayonne ham and rocket

SERVES 6

Annie Bell, cook and food writer, who wrote *Living and Eating* with John Pawson, commutes between London and her house in Normandy, the inspiration for this recipe of figs, ham and rocket. 'In Normandy we have a local artisanal ham to call on. Like Bayonne ham, it is cut into lusciously thick slices, a more robust product than its Italian cousins, and a slice or two is normally enough. You can dish this one up as an appetiser or starter while you're cooking the main course.'

1 tablespoon balsamic vinegar

6 tablespoons extra-virgin olive oil, plus a little extra

6 figs, stalks trimmed and halved

12 slices Bayonne ham

6 handfuls of wild rocket

Whisk the balsamic vinegar with some seasoning in a small bowl, then whisk in the 6 tablespoons of oil. Brush the fig halves with oil, and barbecue flesh-side down for 3–5 minutes until caramelised, then turn and grill for another 3 minutes. Remove them to a plate and leave to cool for 5 minutes. Lay a couple of slices of Bayonne ham on the side of six plates, with a pile of rocket beside. Place two fig halves on this side of the salad, and drizzle the dressing over the ham, rocket and figs. If you have to cook indoors because of the weather, heat a double-ridged griddle over a medium-low heat and grill the figs flesh-side down for 3 minutes until caramelised, then turn and grill the other side for about 1 minute or so until the figs feel soft when gently squeezed with a pair of tongs. The wild rocket that has crept into the shops as the new leaf in town is to be lauded over the ordinary. The leaves have a defined bite, but are that much more delicate in appearance.

Griddled courgette, pine nut and raisin salad by Sophie Grigson

450 g medium-size courgettes

6 tablespoons extra-virgin olive oil

30 g raisins

30 g pine nuts, lightly toasted

2 tablespoons chopped fennel or dill

2 tablespoons lemon juice

Preheat a griddle pan (or barbecue grill) until very hot. Cut the courgettes into two or three, then halve or quarter each piece lengthways depending on size. Toss with 2 tablespoons of oil until all the pieces are thoroughly coated. Griddle or barbecue for a few minutes on each side, until striped with brown and tender. Mix with the remaining ingredients and leave to cool. Taste and adjust the seasoning and serve at room temperature.

Sam and Sam's chicken salad

SERVES 4

This is the chicken salad devised by Sam and Sam Clark who run Moro Restaurant in Exmouth Market. It is the essence of simplicity and tastes terrific.

4 organic, free-range chicken breasts

400 g green beans, tailed

16 sweet cherry tomatoes, sliced in half (or any other good quality tomato)

4 tablespoons flatleaf parsley (or coriander), roughly chopped

for the dressing

1 tablespoon lemon juice

4 tablespoons olive oil

for the chicken marinade

2 cloves of garlic, crushed to a paste with salt

juice of half a lemon

2 tablespoons olive oil

2 teaspoons whole cumin seeds, lightly pan-roasted and then roughly ground

1 teaspoon sweet paprika

Mix all the marinade ingredients together and rub all over the chicken. Leave for up to 6 hours.

Whisk the ingredients for the dressing together with some sea salt and black pepper; check the seasoning and then set aside. Bring a large saucepan of salted water to the boil and add the green beans. Boil for 2–3 minutes until just tender but not al dente. Drain well, then place in a large salad bowl along with the tomatoes and parsley. Set aside. Grill or fry the chicken until cooked through but still juicy. Let it rest for 3–5 minutes, slice and add to the salad bowl. Pour over the dressing, toss well and serve immediately.

Adeline Yen Mah's recipe for Auntie Ada's tofu salad

SERVES 2-3

Adeline Yen Mah, the best-selling author and doctor, explains the Chinese view of healthy food. She uses ingredients which the Chinese classify as 'bu' or nutritious. Her personal definition of 'bu' is food that is not just nourishing but actively healthy. This salad is designed along these lines: 'it contains tofu with coriander, spring onions, ginger, pickled onions and walnuts with a little bit of soy sauce and sesame oil – ginger is good. It has a lot of antioxidants, as do green vegetables such as coriander. Walnuts have omega-3 fatty acids. There is no cholesterol. Tofu has beneficial ingredients.'

225 g block of soft tofu

½ teaspoon sesame oil

60 g shredded red ginger

60 g shredded pickled scallions

80 g julienned green onions

80 g coriander leaves

60 g walnut pieces

1 tablespoon Maggi (or Kikkoman) soy sauce

Slice the tofu block in half horizontally, then cut into 2 cm cubes. Sprinkle the tofu freely with salt. Drizzle soy sauce and sesame oil on to the surface and spread evenly with the back of a spoon. Sprinkle the ginger, scallions, green onions and coriander on top (in that order). Add the walnut pieces and serve chilled.

An English lettuce salad

SERVES 4

Simon Hopkinson's plea for some sanity to return to the art of domestic cooking is encapsulated in his recipe for an old-fashioned English lettuce salad, 'quite superb when done with care', he notes, but 'quite abominable when carelessly thrown together'.

6 hard-boiled eggs, separated; the yolks sieved into a bowl, the whites coarsely chopped

for the salad cream

3 teaspoons sugar

salt and cayenne pepper

2 teaspoons English mustard

1½ teaspoons tarragon vinegar

300 ml whipping cream

1 tablespoon fresh tarragon, coarsely chopped

for the salad

hearts of some very fresh round lettuces, separated into leaves, washed and dried

12 thin spanking-fresh spring onions, trimmed and sliced into 3-cm lengths

12 radishes, washed, halved and put into ice-cold water for 30 minutes

half a cucumber, peeled and not too thinly sliced

a few leaves of mint, torn to shreds

To make the dressing: whisk together the sieved egg yolks, sugar, seasoning, mustard and vinegar. Add the cream and tarragon and mix thoroughly. Arrange the ingredients for the salad in a large shallow dish, achieving as natural a look as possible. Sprinkle over the chopped egg whites and then spoon over the cream dressing in dribbles and swirls. Serve the salad straight away.

Herb, leaf and flower salad

Paul Hughes who runs Howbarrow Farm in Cumbria, an organic herb garden specialising in unusual varieties of herbs and plants, likes to make his own herb oils and vinegars, using different combinations of herbs – hyssop and mint, or tarragon and purple basil; 'whatever seems good'. This one of the Howbarrow salads.

wild rocket

salad rocket

French parsley

buckler leaf sorrel

blood-veined sorrel

nasturtium flowers

borage flowers

pot marigold flowers

chive flowers

Combine all the leaves and flowers together, and serve with a vinaigrette of 3 tablespoons oil, 1 tablespoon vinegar, 1 teaspoon honey, and fresh herbs – unless using herb vinegar.
To make a herb vinegar: put a quantity of good quality white wine vinegar in a jam jar, stuff it full of herbs, leave on a sunny windowsill for 2 weeks, strain and bottle.
To make a herb oil: put the best extra-virgin olive oil you can afford in a jar, stuff full of herbs, making sure that the herbs are covered in oil to prevent mould, and keep covered.

Grated carrot and poppy seed salad with lime juice

Sarah Raven runs the Cutting Garden in East Sussex, growing and cooking all her own food. 'This is one of the tastiest ways to eat large, maincrop carrots. Peel them, grate them and mix with a simple dressing and seeds. It has a lovely nutty flavour, with sweetness from the carrots and sharpness from the lime, and is particularly good with Indian food or gooey French cheese and bread.'

2 tablespoons extra-virgin olive oil

juice and zest of 1 lime

3–4 large carrots, peeled and grated

1 tablespoon poppy seeds, dry-fried for 5 minutes

1 red salad onion, sliced thinly ('I use North Holland Blood Red Redmate which is an excellent companion plant to grow with carrots to avoid carrot root fly')

salt and freshly ground black pepper

Mix the oil with the lime and salt and pepper in the base of a large salad bowl. Put the carrots in on top, then the still-hot seeds and the onion. Mix together and serve.

Salad of Napa Valley heirloom tomatoes, San Marzano tomato marmalade, grilled red onions and Greek basil

SERVES 6

Thomas Keller, who owns the French Laundry, one of the top 50 restaurants in the world, has this recipe for a glut of late summer tomatoes. 'During the summer months, the tomatoes in our garden are overabundant. I like to use them fresh off the vine and simply dressed with Armando Manni Per Me extra-virgin olive oil, balsamic vinegar and Greek basil. I also love to make tomato marmalade which we continue to enjoy months after the tomato season is over.'

36 assorted small vine-ripened tomatoes

2 medium-size sweet red onions, peeled and sliced 10-cm thick

extra-virgin olive oil (Armando Manni Per Me, if possible), as required

balsamic vinegar, as required

enough Greek basil leaves to garnish tomatoes

country bread, grilled

tomato marmalade (see recipe below)

For the tomatoes: use a sharp knife to first core the tops then score the opposite end. Drop the tomatoes in boiling water for 15 seconds then plunge them quickly into ice water. Remove and peel skins. Set aside.

For the onions: in a small bowl, lightly coat the onions with the oil and season with salt and pepper. Grill the onions until the inside has turned soft and translucent. Set aside.

To serve: slice the peeled tomatoes and arrange on a serving platter. Season with the olive oil, vinegar, salt, freshly ground black pepper and Greek basil. Leave to rest for at least 30 minutes before serving to allow the flavours to marry. Add the grilled onions and serve with oil, vinegar, nicely grilled country bread and tomato marmalade on the side.

Tomato marmalade

MAKES 500 G

250 g red wine vinegar (Keller measures liquids by weight)

100 g sugar

1 kg vine-ripened tomatoes, peeled, de-seeded and minced

120 g shallots, chopped

60 g red onions, chopped

Begin by making a gastrique. Put the vinegar and sugar in a medium-sized pot and reduce to a thick syrup consistency. Add the tomatoes, shallots and onions and stir continuously until all liquid has evaporated and the mixture has become thick. This will keep for up to 2 weeks in the refrigerator.

Pasta and Rice
Sepia pasta with prawns and chilli
by Annie Bell

SERVES 4

So beautiful to look at you can hardly bring yourself to eat it – noodles dyed black with sepia ink relish, the presence of pink shellfish. Here it's prawns, but it could just as well be crab or squid.

250 g sepia noodles

8 tablespoons extra-virgin olive oil

3 cloves of garlic, peeled and finely chopped

I medium-hot red chilli, finely chopped

350 g shelled raw tiger prawns

3 tablespoons white wine

juice of I lemon

8 heaped tablespoons coarsely chopped flatleaf parsley

Bring a large pan of salted water to the boil. Add the pasta, give it a stir and cook until just tender. The time this will take depends on the type of noodles, so check the packet for the ideal cooking time. At the same time, heat 6 tablespoons of the olive oil in a large frying pan over a high heat, add the garlic, chilli and prawns, and cook, turning them for about a minute until they are a nice shrimp pink, seasoning them as you go. Add the wine and cook for about a minute more until the wine reduces a little, then remove from the heat. Drain the pasta into a colander and return it to the saucepan. Tip in the contents of the frying pan and toss. Add the lemon juice, remaining olive oil and the flatleaf parsley and toss again. Taste for seasoning and serve straight away.

Ravioloni con radicchio e ricotta

This recipe for ravioli stuffing was taught to a group of students on a Gourmet on Tour shopping and cooking course in Tuscany. It is devised by Carla Tomasi, one-time chef at Frith in London, and is quite the most delicious ravioli ever tasted. The following quantities should fill shop-bought or homemade ravioli for six people.

I head of radicchio, Trevisano, Castelfranco or Verona, shredded quite thinly

I red onion, not too small, finely sliced

olive oil

250 g good quality ricotta

enough Parmesan to bind the mixture, usually about 60 g

Fry the radicchio and onion gently in olive oil until they have wilted and the moisture from the pan has evaporated. Tip into a mixing bowl and leave to cool. Then add the ricotta, Parmesan and season. Use as required. This is a wet filling, so do not fill the ravioli too early as it will leak; alternatively you may fill the ravioli and then freeze them. If unfrozen, boil for about 2 minutes. If cooking from frozen, drop them in boiling water still frozen and cook them for not less than 4 minutes on a medium heat (a fast boil will cause them to burst open). Drain and serve.

Alice Waters' tomato confit for pasta

Alice Waters, the pioneering Californian chef, gained much of her culinary inspiration from cooking for her daughter. This is her recipe for tomato confit for pasta.

basil leaves

ripe tomatoes (about 2 per serving), peeled, halved and de-seeded

extra-virgin olive oil

Preheat the oven to 180°C/Gas Mark 4. Make a bed of basil leaves in the bottom of an ovenproof dish that will hold the tomatoes snugly in one layer. Place the tomatoes core side down on the basil. Season lightly. Pour in enough extra-virgin olive oil to come halfway up the sides of the tomatoes. Bake for 1½ hours in the oven, until the tomatoes are soft and lightly caramelised and have infused the oil with their perfume. Season to taste and serve spooned over cooked and drained fresh noodles.

Pasta with sardines

SERVES 6

This dish was served by fashion designer Luisa Beccaria in her Sicilian castle. Castellucio is built round an ancient cobbled courtyard whose walls are covered in roses. In the evening Luisa's husband Lucio makes Campari with Sicilian blood oranges – 'red like the Etna volcano, while his wife and daughters surround him in dresses the colour of moonshine and silvery starlight, all designed by his wife'.

900 g fresh sardines

2 tablespoons olive oil

2 medium-size onions, finely chopped

3 cloves of garlic, finely chopped

2 small dried chillies, crumbled

3 anchovies, tinned or fresh

50 g sultanas soaked in water

2 tablespoons basil leaves, finely chopped

half a glass of white wine

8 tablespoons passata

250 g spaghetti or penne rigate

2 fennel bulbs, tops chopped, bulbs finely sliced

50 g pine nuts

110 g breadcrumbs, fried in olive oil

Gut the sardines, remove the head, tail and backbone and flour the fish. Heat the oil in a pan big enough to fit in all the sardines in one layer. Fry the onions and garlic, then add the chillies, anchovies, sultanas and basil, and place the sardines on top. Add the wine and passata and cook briefly. Don't stir too much. Cook the pasta and fennel in a pan of boiling, salted water. Drain and add to the sardines. Season and sprinkle with the pine nuts, breadcrumbs and extra chilli if required.

Fish and Shellfish
Grilled squid with chillies

SERVES 6

By Ruth Rogers and Rose Gray, served at the River Cafe in Hammersmith – 'the easy white sweetness of squid brought to life with the fire of red chilli and the pepper of rocket'.

6 medium-size squid, no bigger than your hand

12 large fresh red chillies, de-seeded and very finely chopped

extra-virgin olive oil

225 g rocket leaves

3 lemons, quartered

for the oil and lemon dressing

6 tablespoons extra-virgin olive oil

2 tablespoons lemon juice

Mix the dressing ingredients together, season to taste and add more lemon if you wish. Clean the squid by cutting the body open to make a flat piece. Scrape out the guts, keeping the tentacles in their bunches but removing the eyes and mouth. Using a serrated knife, score the inner side of the flattened squid body with parallel lines about 1 cm apart, and then do the same thing in the other direction to make cross-hatching. To make the sauce, put the chopped chilli in a bowl and cover with about 2.5 cm of the oil. Season with salt and pepper.

Place the squid (including the tentacles) scored side down on a very hot grill, season with salt and pepper and grill for 1–2 minutes. Turn the squid pieces over; they will immediately curl up, by which time they will be cooked. Toss the rocket in the dressing. Arrange a squid body and tentacles on each plate with some rocket. Place a little of the chilli on the squid and serve with lemon quarters.

Tomato and salmon koulibiak

SERVES 4–6

This recipe uses sunblush tomatoes and is a take on the Russian fish pie – to eat cold at a picnic or hot for supper with a herb salad.

360 g ready-made shortcrust pastry

2 tablespoons tomato purée

600 g fresh organic smoked salmon

6 tablespoons sunblush tomatoes, drained of oil and chopped

4 tablespoons cream cheese

2 cloves of garlic, crushed to a paste

2 sprigs of parsley, chopped

2 sprigs of basil, chopped

leaves from 2 sprigs of tarragon, chopped

1 egg, beaten with 1 tablespoon of milk

Preheat the oven to 230°C/Gas Mark 8. Roll the pastry into a large rectangle, about 2 cm thick, and lay across an oiled baking tray.

Spread the surface with the tomato purée. Tear the salmon into large pieces and lay them in the centre of the pastry, covering an area of about 25 cm by 10 cm. Scatter the chopped tomatoes on top. Mix the cream cheese with the garlic and herbs and spread lightly on top of the tomatoes. Season with salt and freshly ground black pepper, wrap the pastry around the filling and seal together using the beaten egg mixture as glue. Brush the surface of the koulibiak with the remaining egg and bake for 20 minutes until the pastry is crisp and golden. Allow to cool on the tray slightly before slicing.

Spicy barbecued langoustines
with lemon and garlic

SERVES 4

A good fishmonger should be able to order
live langoustines for you. See page 204
for suppliers of sake if you have difficulty
obtaining it.

8 large live langoustines

1 tablespoon chopped fennel leaves

for the dressing

100 ml sake

**2 tablespoons Japanese soy sauce (Kikkoman is
best)**

1 heaped teaspoon garlic purée

½ teaspoon cayenne pepper

1 teaspoon grated ginger

3 tablespoons freshly squeezed lemon juice

4 tablespoons olive oil

Mix the dressing ingredients well and store in the
fridge. Lay the langoustines on their back and use
a large sharp knife or cleaver to cut them in half
down the centre. Arrange on a grill rack (hinged
barbecue racks are best for this job) and season
with salt and pepper. Grill or barbecue for 4–6
minutes until just cooked – overcooking destroys
the wonders of langoustine, which should have a
meaty, springy texture. Drench well with the sauce
and fennel and devour while still hot.

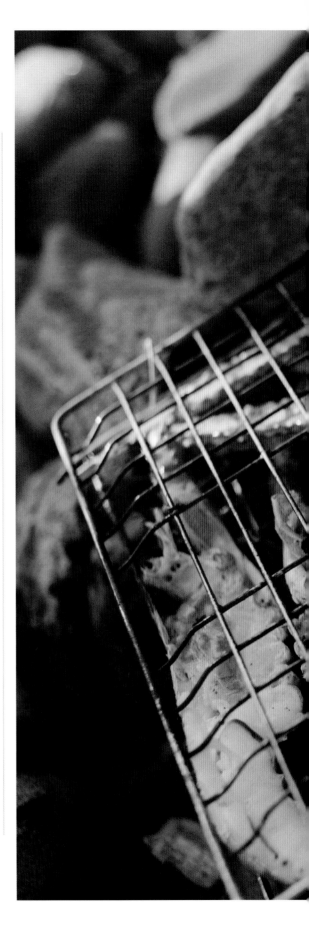

Ceviche of minted scallops
with pink grapefruit

SERVES 4

Carolyn Robb was chef to the Prince of Wales for 11 years; her role was to spirit up food for wherever he happened to be. 'I could never have anticipated the unpredictability of each day,' she says. 'It was not a job for a chef with a big ego.' She cooked this dish for Lisa Faulkner the actress, and Tara Palmer Tomkinson.

12 scallops (off the shell, coral removed)

100 ml freshly squeezed lime juice

100 ml fresh pink grapefruit juice

2 teaspoons salt

100 g fresh mint leaves, cut into long thin strips

2 serrano chillies, sliced very thinly diagonally (you can use jalapenos)

half a red onion, finely sliced

2 pink grapefruit, peeled and cut into thin segments (for garnish)

8 thin slices of grilled crispy pancetta (optional)

Place the scallops on a baking tray lined with baking parchment, cover with clingfilm and freeze for about an hour until the scallops are firm but not frozen solid. Blend all the remaining ingredients except the grapefruit segments and pancetta in a non-metallic bowl. Remove the scallops from the freezer, two or three at a time, and slice thinly. Gently mix the scallops into the fruit juice. Refrigerate for about 2 hours, until the scallops turn an opaque white colour. Serve on a platter or in a glass, garnished with the grapefruit segments and the pancetta.

Pan-fried prawns with Pernod

SERVES 1

This is Franck Leibeiz's spectacular flaming prawn dish that he cooked one night on a Provençal chateau terrace overlooking the vines sweeping down to the sea. The fire was scented with vine wood.

1 tablespoon olive oil

150 g prawns

2 cloves of garlic, freshly crushed

½ glass of Pernod

Heat the olive oil in a deep frying-pan, and throw in the prawns (still in their shells) with the garlic and some salt and pepper.

Sauté the prawns until they have a wonderful autumn leaf colour (this will take 5–6 minutes). At the end, add the Pernod and enflame by tilting one side of the pan into the edge of the flame until it catches and the alcohol burns off. This can also be achieved with a lighted match.

Roasted lobster salad

Aga guru Amy Willcock devised this recipe for sailing picnics at her Isle of Wight home. 'Lobsters, vacuum-packed by Mother Nature and impervious to squashing, make the perfect boating food.'

6 x 1 kg lobsters, alive

a little grapeseed oil

2 yellow peppers, roasted, de-seeded and sliced

1 red pepper, roasted, de-seeded and sliced

2 ripe avocados, cut into cubes

1 small cucumber, peeled, de-seeded and diced

2 tablespoons sunblush tomatoes, chopped

1 tablespoon pitted black olives, sliced in half

1 bag of mixed baby salad leaves

for the lemon and basil dressing

1 teaspoon Dijon mustard

juice of 1 lemon

grated zest of 1 lemon

6 tablespoons olive oil

2 tablespoons basil leaves, freshly shredded

Combine all the dressing ingredients in a bowl and whisk together. Set aside. (It can be made a few days in advance.) Put the live lobsters on a chopping board, insert the point of a sharp knife hard into the back of the head and push down to kill the lobster. Cut the lobster in half, straight down the middle of the back. Remove any green intestines. Lay the lobsters in a large, preheated shallow roasting tin and drizzle over a little grapeseed oil. Roast them in a preheated oven, 220°C/Gas Mark 7 (the roasting oven on the second set of runners for Agas) for 10–15 minutes. Remove them from the oven and cool. Take the lobster out of its shell, de-vein the tails and remove the claw meat in one piece, reserving to one side. Chop the lobster into cubes, and combine it in a large bowl with the peppers, avocados, cucumber, tomatoes, olives and all but 2 tablespoons of dressing. Toss together and let stand for 10–15 minutes, then toss again. This can be done earlier in the day. Spread the salad leaves on a large platter and drizzle over the remaining dressing. Spoon the lobster mix on top of the leaves and garnish with the reserved claws and some basil leaves. Serve this with hot new potatoes.

Baked fish with vine-ripened tomatoes by Jane Packer

SERVES 4

500–750 g whole fish, such as sea bass

fresh garden herbs, such as parsley, thyme and sage, chopped

olive oil

225 g vine tomatoes

2 unwaxed organic lemons

Preheat the oven to 180°C/Gas Mark 4. Gut the fish or ask your fishmonger to do it for you. Stuff the fish with the selection of chopped herbs, and season and douse with olive oil. Place in a large roasting tray with the vine tomatoes. Quarter the lemons and, leaving the skin on, put them into the roasting tray. Simply roast for 20–30 minutes until the fish is tender and cooked.

Grilled sea bream with lemon and bay leaves by Franck Leibeiz

SERVES 1

The kind of fish dish you can also cook on a beach using nothing but a fire and a few bay leaves.

1 sea bream (400–500 g)

1 peeled lemon, sliced

2 bay leaves

2 sticks dried fennel

Ask your fishmonger to prepare (gut, de-scale etc.) the fish. At home, make vertical incisions on both sides of the fish in which to insert the peeled lemon slices and the bay leaves. Stuff the dry fennel into the open stomach. Place the fish on a very hot grill and cook for 4 minutes on each side, until the skin has crisped and browned. Season lightly with salt and pepper and finish cooking the fish in the oven for 5 minutes at 150°C/Gas Mark 2.

Shell-on prawns with scrumpy butter by Rose Prince

SERVES 4

Adrian Sellick is the last mudhorseman on Bridgewater Bay – he wades through two foot of soft mud a mile out into the Severn Estuary to reach his fishing nets full of prawns. He and his father sell the prawns from the village shop at Stolford. This is the Sellick recipe for prawns and butter. You can substitute strong dry cider for the scrumpy if you wish.

4 pints of shell-on pink prawns, or brown shrimps

I shallot, chopped

75 ml scrumpy or cider

2 blades of mace

180 g unsalted English butter, cut into chunks

Place equal amounts of prawns in four bowls. Put the shallot in a pan with the cider and the mace. Place over the heat and bring to the boil and allow to cook until reduced by half. Sieve the contents of the pan, reserving the liquid. Put the liquid back into the pan with one piece of the mace and place over the heat. Whisk in the butter, piece by piece until you have a smooth yellow sauce. Add salt to taste and a little black pepper. Divide among four small dishes and serve as a dipping sauce for the prawns as you peel them.

Sea bass with coriander yogurt sauce and lemon purée

SERVES 6

This is Tom Aikens' recipe for a summer dinner party.

6 lemons

sugar

I bunch of coriander

400 g natural Greek yogurt

I cucumber

olive oil

6 x 70 g pieces of sea bass

Cut five of the lemons lengthways into quarters, slice them thinly and put them in a pan. Cover with water and cook over a medium heat until there is only a little liquid left. Purée in a blender, adding a tablespoon of sugar and the juice from half of the sixth lemon (add more sugar to taste). Set aside. Put three-quarters of the coriander and the yogurt in the blender and purée, adding a little lemon juice, salt and a pinch of sugar. Set aside. Cut the cucumber in half, slice very thinly and mix with the rest of the coriander and a drizzle of olive oil. Season to taste and add a pinch of sugar. Set aside.

Heat a drizzle of olive oil in a non-stick frying pan. Season the fish and place in the pan skin side down. Cook for 3–4 minutes until golden round the edges. While this is cooking, divide the coriander sauce among six bowls, add the cucumber salad then three dots of the lemon purée. Turn the fish and cook for a further minute, squeeze on a little lemon juice, remove from the pan and place on top of the cucumber.

Meat, Poultry and Game
Sausage tart with onion marmalade

SERVES 6

This sausage tart is a favourite with Amy Willcock's daughters, 'the caramelised onion marmalade along with breadcrumbs and cream makes a delicious sweet and sour filling'. The recipe was inspired by the 'sausage tart and marmalade rolls' in *'Chitty Chitty Bang Bang'*.

20.5 cm loose-bottomed tart tin lined with savoury shortcrust pastry (bought if you don't have the time – Saxby's is good)

6 Duchy Original old-fashioned pork sausages

60 g fresh breadcrumbs

2 tablespoons double cream

I teaspoon dry mustard powder, heaped

2 large whole eggs

for the onion marmalade

sunflower oil

I heaped tablespoon good, chunky-cut marmalade

2 red onions, thinly sliced

First make the onion marmalade. Heat a little of the sunflower oil – about a tablespoon – and the marmalade in a frying-pan, toss in the onion and cook gently over a medium heat until the onions are caramelised and thick. Season. This will take about 10–15 minutes. If you have an Aga cook it on the floor of the roasting oven. While the onions are cooking down, blind-bake the pastry for 10 minutes in a preheated oven at 190°C/Gas Mark 5. Remove and cool a little. Cook the sausages for 10 minutes or until they start to brown in a frying-pan on the hob, under a grill or on the first set of runners in the Aga. When you are ready

to assemble your tart, spread the onion marmalade on the bottom of the pastry. Mix the breadcrumbs, cream, mustard powder and eggs together and season. Pour this over the onion marmalade in the tart.

Split your sausages horizontally and arrange them on top. Cook the tart in a preheated oven, 180°C/Gas Mark 4 for 20–25 minutes or until golden. Eat hot or cold with more mustard. For Agas, there is no need to blind bake the pastry. Assemble as above and cook on the floor of the roasting oven with the cold plain shelf above for 20–25 minutes or until golden.

Lamb with peas, broad beans, artichoke hearts and roast garlic

SERVES 6

Tom Aikens' recipe for lamb and summer vegetables.

2 kg fresh peas shelled
1 kg broad beans shelled
300 g sprue asparagus
3 bulbs new season garlic
olive oil
1 bunch thyme
3 baby artichokes
12 shallots, peeled
150 g butter
1 teaspoon sugar
2 lamb loins
100 ml double cream
1 lemon
1 small bunch basil, cut finely
4 punnets of fresh pea shoots

Preheat the oven to 170°C/Gas Mark 3. Cook the peas for 2 minutes in boiling salted water and refresh in iced water. Cook the broad beans for 1 minute and refresh in iced water. In clean boiling water, cook the asparagus for 2 minutes and refresh in iced water. Remove the outer skin of the broad beans. Cut the garlic bulbs in half and place cut side down in a frying pan with olive oil and a little thyme. Sprinkle with sea salt and cook slowly until golden. Place in the oven for 5 minutes.

With each artichoke, peel the stalk, remove the outer layers of the heart and cut a little of the top off. Cut in half lengthways then place face down in the pan on a low heat with olive oil. Sprinkle with sea salt and cook slowly until golden on one side,

then repeat on the other. Place the shallots in a pan and just cover with water, add 75 g of the butter, the sugar and a little thyme. Bring to a simmer then cook until tender, slowly reducing the liquor by about half. Leave to cool.

Turn down the oven to 160°C/Gas Mark 2. Season the lamb and seal in a hot pan until golden and then place them in the oven on a wire rack for 5 minutes. Remove and leave to rest for at least 5–10 minutes. Reheat the shallots, add the cream, a squeeze of lemon juice and reduce a little. Add the peas, broad beans and 75 g of butter. Season to taste.

Reheat the lamb in the oven. Add the asparagus and basil to the peas and broad beans. Divide among six plates. Slice the lamb, place on the peas and arrange the artichoke and roast garlic alongside. Dress the pea shoots in olive oil, a little lemon juice and sea salt and place on the lamb.

Beef tartare and horseradish

with wood sorrel, tarragon and juniper
berries

SERVES 4

René Redzepi, the chef at Noma, the
Copenhagen restaurant that has made it into
the world top 50, suggests eating this variation
of the raw beef dish with your bare hands.
Sorrel takes just two or three weeks to grow in
a bed or pot but is sometimes available from
specialist grocers. Alternatively, try a peppery
leaf such as rocket or even cress instead of the
lemon-flavoured sorrel. The aniseed taste of
basil would not be suitable. Naturally reared,
well-hung beef is essential for the success of
this recipe.

300 g prime fillet of beef

2 thin slices of rye bread, chopped and fried
until crisp (pumpernickel is the closest
alternative to Danish rye bread)

2 tablespoons horseradish, freshly grated

handful of wood sorrel leaves

1 small onion or 2 shallots, very thinly sliced

about 16 juniper berries, ground in a pestle and
mortar or crushed with a rolling pin

for the tarragon emulsion

6 sprigs of tarragon

1 tablespoon white wine vinegar

1 tablespoon chicken stock/water

½ shallot

½ clove of garlic

150 ml oil

sea salt

lemon juice

Begin with the tarragon emulsion: mix the first six
ingredients in a liquidiser, blending to a smooth
cream. Season to taste with salt and a few drops of
lemon juice then refrigerate.

Using a very sharp knife, 'scrape' the meat into
fine strips and divide among four plates. Sprinkle
with salt, the rye bread and horseradish and finish
off with the wood sorrel and sliced onion. Put a
spoonful of the emulsion beside the meat, then the
juniper in a small pile next to it. Eat the dish with
your fingers, taking a pinch of the raw meat and
dipping it first in the emulsion, then in the spice.

Confit of artichokes, fondant potato and wilted Good King Henry with roast venison and a lavender jus

SERVES 4

The kitchen garden at Swinton Park is run by Susan Cunliffe-Lister who provides the kitchen with a constant supply of organic, fresh produce. One hundred years ago, the garden fed the family and a staff of 50. Artichokes, first introduced from France in the 16th century were still grown there in the 19th century. 'I was very keen on growing them again,' says Susan. Good King Henry is a weed that you wilt down like spinach. It grows in one of the borders with mint, angelica, chives, lemon balm, sorrel, fennel and parsley.

for the confit of artichokes

12 globe artichokes, stalks removed

1 garlic bulb

1 bay leaf

1 sprig of rosemary

1 sprig of thyme

1 tablespoon whole peppercorns

500 ml extra-virgin olive oil

Put the artichokes, crushed garlic bulb, bay leaf, rosemary, thyme and peppercorns in an oven dish and cover with the olive oil. Place in the oven at 110°C/Gas Mark ¼ for 20–30 minutes or until tender to touch. Remove from the oven. When cool, remove from the oil, drain off the excess liquid and pick away the outer leaves down the 'heart'. Set aside and keep warm in the oven.

for the fondant potato

500 g butter

4 large whole potatoes, peeled and cut into large chunks as though for roasting

Melt the butter in a pan and submerge the potatoes. Cook over a gentle heat until soft. Keep warm in the oven.

for the wilted Good King Henry

800 g Good King Henry (or spinach), stalks removed

100 g butter

Warm a pan and melt the butter. Add the leaves, then season. Remove the pan from the heat when the leaves have wilted, drain the leaves and wrap in a tea towel to dry.

for the roast venison

1 small venison haunch, approx 140 g per person

1 teaspoon vegetable oil

Heat a pan over a moderate heat and add the vegetable oil. Season the haunch, then sear the meat until golden brown on all sides (this should take 4–5 minutes). Finish under a hot grill for about 10 minutes until tender to touch. Allow to rest for 10 minutes. Thinly slice, serving pink in the centre.

for the lavender jus

1 small onion, diced

1 carrot, roughly chopped

1 leek, roughly chopped

1 celery stick, roughly chopped

1 bay leaf

1 sprig of thyme

600 ml beef stock

8 lavender leaves

Place all the ingredients apart from the lavender in a large pan. Bring to the boil and simmer for 1–2 hours then cool. Strain the liquid from the pan, removing all the vegetables. Return the liquid to the heat for 20 minutes, reducing by two-thirds, then add the lavender leaves for 4 minutes and remove before serving.

To serve: place a portion of the Good King Henry on the side of the plate. Layer on top of this the thinly sliced venison. Cut the potato into rings with a cylinder cutter and place on the side of the plate. Place four artichoke hearts around the side of the venison. Drizzle the jus around the venison, potato and artichokes on the edge of the plate.

Chicken breast with morels, spinach and dry sherry
by Raymond Blanc

SERVES 4

25 g dried morels, soaked for a minimum of 1 hour in 250 ml of water

4 free-range skinless chicken breasts (180 g each)

1 tablespoon unsalted butter

250 g button mushrooms, very firm, washed quickly and quartered

120 ml dry sherry, boiled for 30 seconds to remove the alcohol

400 ml double cream

for the spinach

2 tablespoons unsalted butter

400 g spinach leaves, tough stalks removed, well washed

Drain the morels, reserving the water. Strain the water through a fine sieve or muslin and set aside. Then wash the morels in plenty of water to remove any sand. Drain again, and squeeze any excess water from the morels. Season the chicken breasts with sea salt and pepper. In a frying-pan, melt the butter over a medium heat until it is foaming. Add the chicken, seal and colour lightly for 3 minutes on each side, remove from the pan and reserve. In the remaining fat, soften the morels and button mushrooms for 1–2 minutes and season with a pinch of sea salt. Add the boiled sherry, 100 ml of the morel water and the double cream. Bring to the boil and place the chicken back in the pan. The sauce must cover the breasts. Lower the heat to a gentle simmer and cook for 13–15 minutes depending on the size of the breasts. Remove the chicken from the pan and keep warm.

To finish: reduce the sauce for 6–8 minutes on full heat until it thickens and coats the back of a spoon. Reduce the heat and place the chicken breasts into the sauce to reheat for 2 minutes. Season.

To cook the spinach: in a large saucepan, melt the butter and add the spinach leaves. Lightly season with sea salt and freshly ground black pepper. Cover and cook over a high heat for 2 minutes. Remove the lid, stir and cook for a further minute. Season and arrange on a plate with the chicken. Spoon the sauce and mushrooms over.

Georgian coronation chicken

SERVES 4

Nino Toradze hosted a Georgian feast one summer in honour of her friend Theresa Tollemache. She produced a traditional Caucasus mountain picnic: kebabs, Georgian coronation chicken, organic herbs grown in her Suffolk garden and a table sprinkled with nasturtium flowers. 'This is really nothing like coronation chicken but it is a simple, cold chicken dish ("bazha" in Georgian) which travels well,' she says. 'It's perfect for picnics and uses pomegranate seeds instead of sultanas. Most Georgian dishes take a long time to cook and prepare but this is one exception. It is worth going to the trouble of juicing your own pomegranates (using a juicer) if you can't find the juice at the supermarket (try Waitrose and Budgens for POM Wonderful Pomegranate Juice). Be generous with the herbs and eat the finished article at room temperature. You can also make this dish with white fish but use only water for soaking the walnuts, omitting the pomegranate juice.'

200 g walnuts
I clove of garlic, roughly chopped
pomegranate juice
4 teaspoons dried coriander
a pinch of red chilli powder
4 teaspoons salt
4 cold chicken breasts (or equivalent), grilled, barbecued or poached
seeds from I pomegranate

Grind the walnuts and the garlic clove in a food processor. Tip the resulting paste into a jug and cover with a half-and-half mixture of pomegranate juice and water until the liquid comes to I cm over the top of the walnut mix. It should look like a thin purée. Add the coriander, chilli and salt and mix in the food processor until it resembles a thick paste. Slice the chicken and layer it in a shallow dish. Completely cover the chicken with sauce and leave the sauce to soak in for at least several hours. Remove from the fridge at least I hour before eating and sprinkle with pomegranate seeds just before serving.

Vegetables
Red peppers stuffed with Gorgonzola

SERVES 6

This is Annie Bell's recipe for stuffed peppers: 'The sweetness of the peppers is a great match for the creamy melted blue cheese. Fourme d'Ambert would be another good candidate, as would Roquefort. Go for average-size peppers rather than large.'

extra-virgin olive oil

1 Spanish onion, peeled and chopped

2 red peppers, core and seeds removed, diced

1 tablespoon balsamic vinegar

250 g Gorgonzola. diced

75 g fresh white breadcrumbs

2 tablespoons coarsely chopped flatleaf parsley

2 tablespoons coarsely chopped mint

8 long pointed red peppers

Heat 2 tablespoons of extra-virgin olive oil in a large frying pan over a medium heat, add the onion and diced peppers, season and sauté for 10 minutes until soft, stirring occasionally. Sprinkle over half the balsamic vinegar, which will evaporate almost immediately. Remove to a large bowl and leave to cool. Stir in the cheese, breadcrumbs and herbs. Trim the stalks of the eight pointed peppers, leaving about 2 cm, then cut the tops off but don't throw them away. Remove any seeds inside. Stuff with the pepper-and-cheese mixture, pushing it well down to the bottom of each pepper. Arrange the stuffed peppers with their lids in place in a roasting dish. The peppers can be prepared to this point up to a couple of hours in advance. Heat the oven to 220°C/Gas Mark 7. Drizzle a little more oil over the peppers and season, then roast for 25 minutes until golden in patches. Drizzle over the remaining balsamic vinegar and set aside for 15 minutes. Serve warm with the pan juices spooned over.

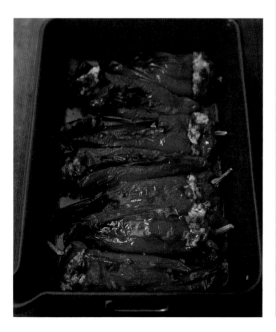

Tumbet

SERVES 4

Stefa Hart, mother of Sam and Eddy Hart who run Fino in London, recalls her mother cooking tumbet, a traditional Majorcan vegetable dish, 'on a fire in the middle of her kitchen floor, which is why the ingredients were traditionally fried. If we wanted anything baked, we took it to the baker and used his oven.' In this version of tumbet, the peppers and potatoes are fried, the aubergines are baked to lessen the oil content.

light olive oil
4 red peppers, sliced and de-seeded
600 g potatoes, sliced into ½ cm discs
2 aubergines, sliced into 1 cm discs, sprinkled with salt and left for 15–20 minutes, then wiped dry
2–3 sprigs of thyme
for the tomato sauce
500 g onions, thinly sliced
500 g ripe tomatoes, quartered
3 cloves of garlic, crushed
2–3 sprigs of thyme

Preheat the oven to 180°C/Gas Mark 4. Heat a little oil in a frying pan and fry the peppers and potatoes separately. Dry on paper towels. Layer the vegetables in an ovenproof serving dish, starting with the potatoes, then the aubergines and lastly the peppers. Season and sprinkle thyme on each layer. Put the tumbet into the oven and bake for 30 minutes.

To make the sauce: fry the onions until soft. Add the tomatoes, garlic and thyme and season with salt and pepper. When the tomatoes are cooked, put the mixture into a blender and blend until smooth. Serve in a separate jug, with the tumbet.

Pea purée

SERVES 4

225 g fresh peas, or frozen will do
knob of butter
chicken stock

Put the peas in boiling chicken stock, boil for one minute and strain. Reserve the stock for future use. Blitz the peas in a food processor, stir in the butter and season with salt and pepper.

Habas fritas con jamón

SERVES 2–4

You can also use fresh or frozen broad beans, which you should cook until they are soft, about 8–10 minutes. The ham is the famous jamón de bellota, made in Andalucia from pigs fed on acorns.

1 tablespoon extra-virgin olive oil
1 clove of garlic, finely chopped
1 jar (390 g) Habitas (Navarrico baby broad beans in olive oil)
100 g cubed Joselito jamón ibérico
2 sprigs of mint

Heat the olive oil in a deep frying pan or wok, add the garlic and fry until brown. Drain the liquid from the jar of beans, or from the cooked fresh beans, and mix the beans with the olive oil and garlic in the pan. Cook on a medium heat for 2–3 minutes until warmed through. Add the cubed ham and the mint and cook for a maximum of 1 minute. Add salt and pepper to taste.

Golden linseed falafel
by Allegra McEvedy

SERVES 6

Between them, Henry Dimbleby and Allegra McEvedy founded Leon, the now rather famous chain of fast food cafes that sells fresh, home-made organic food. Many of their recipes are influenced by Middle Eastern cooking. This is one of them.

250 g chickpeas
1 bunch spring onions, finely chopped
1 medium red onion, grated and the water squeezed out
4 cloves of garlic, peeled and chopped
1 red chilli, finely chopped
4 teaspoons cumin seeds
4 teaspoons ground coriander seeds
30 g flatleaf parsley, chopped
10 g mint leaves, chopped
150 g golden linseeds

Soak the chickpeas overnight in cold water. Preheat the oven to 190°C/Gas Mark 5. Mix together the chickpeas, spring onions, onion, garlic, chilli, cumin, coriander seeds, parsley and mint, and blitz in a blender until smooth. Shape into small flat balls and then roll gently in the linseeds until roughly covered in seeds. Put on a greased baking tray and bake for 15–20 minutes, turning halfway through. Serve warm.

Sauces
Summer sauce

This summer sauce is designed to be eaten with roast meat. There is a winter version as well (see page 187).

leaves from a small bunch each of fresh thyme, rosemary and sage

juice of 2 lemons

200 ml olive oil

3 tablespoons beef stock (ask the butcher for some beef bones, roast them, then cover with water and boil slowly for two hours)

Chop the herbs very finely, add the lemon juice, season with a pinch of sea salt and some freshly ground black pepper, then add the oil. Whisk in the beef stock until it is well blended.

Chilli, pistachio and rose petal sauce

Eat this rich and spicy sauce with marinated lamb that has been roasted or grilled over coals. Nibbed pistachios and dried edible rose petals can be bought from Middle Eastern food shops.

6 tablespoons olive oil

60 g ciabatta or sourdough bread, cut into cubes

2 cloves of garlic, peeled and chopped

2 piquillo or 1 poblano pepper, de-seeded and cut into chunks

6 dried red chillies

2 tablespoons dried edible rose petals

2 tablespoons white wine

150 g nibbed pistachios

1 tablespoon red wine vinegar

Heat the oil in a large pan over a medium heat and fry the cubes of bread until golden. Remove them and set to one side, leaving the oil in the pan, then fry the garlic, peppers and dried chillies until soft. Set aside. Soak the rose petals in the wine. Put them in a food processor with the bread, garlic, peppers, the cooking oil, pistachios and red wine vinegar. Whizz until the sauce is well blended but the colours of the nuts and peppers are still visible. Add more oil if the sauce is too thick.

Parsley, anchovy and black olive sauce

A good sauce for cold pork.

2 tablespoons flatleaf parsley, chopped

2 tablespoons black olives, chopped

juice of half a lemon

1 tablespoon anchovies, chopped

1 tablespoon chopped garlic

6 tablespoons extra-virgin olive oil

1 pinch soft sea salt

Combine all the ingredients and taste for seasoning.

Tomato sauce

Food for Pippa Small, the jewellery designer, has to be uncomplicated. Lightly steamed green beans with olive oil and a twist of lemon, sautéed samphire with onion and garlic, or this delicious tomato sauce, which she serves with couscous. 'Keep the parts separate,' she advises. 'Sauce in one bowl, grain in another, and some harissa, a garlic pounded paste of chillies, to the side.'

1 tablespoon olive oil

1 onion, finely chopped

1 clove of garlic, peeled, but not chopped

2 x 400 g tins of tomatoes or equivalent in fresh tomatoes, peeled, de-seeded and quartered

2 teaspoons sugar

2 teaspoons cumin

2 teaspoons dried coriander

1 small whole chilli

half a lime

5 cm piece of fresh ginger root, peeled

3 tablespoons extra-virgin olive oil

Put the oil in a pan and fry the onion and garlic until they are soft (the garlic can be removed after cooking). Add the tomatoes, sugar, cumin and coriander, chilli and salt to taste. Squeeze in the juice of half a lime, then add the lime skin and ginger root to the sauce (remove the lime, ginger and chilli after cooking). Simmer for 20 minutes, then cool. Whizz in a blender, dribbling in the olive oil. Season.

Puddings
Raspberries with ricotta

SERVES 4

A simple dessert that works very well with almond and polenta crumble. Supermarkets sell pasteurised cow's-milk ricotta. Specialist cheese shops may have fresh sheep-or goat's-milk ricotta. It is usually sold by the slice.

1 organic unwaxed lemon
4 tablespoons caster sugar
4 punnets raspberries
250 g ricotta cheese

Finely grate the lemon zest and mix with the sugar. Leave for a while to allow the flavours to combine. Scatter the raspberries on a large plate, turn the ricotta out of the tub and slice it as finely as possible. Place these ricotta slices over the raspberries. Sprinkle with the lemon sugar.

Raspberry ice-cream by Sarah Raven

SERVES 4

3 tablespoons home-made raspberry jam
500 ml creamy natural yogurt
500 ml single cream
2 medium-size punnets of raspberries

Put all the ingredients into an ice-cream maker and follow its instructions. If you don't have an ice-cream maker, put all the ingredients into a bowl and stir until well mixed and the raspberries are beginning to break up. Spoon into a freezer-proof container and freeze, stirring occasionally to break down any ice crystals.

Gooseberry fool by Allegra McEvedy

SERVES 6

'A mixture of late spring, early summer gooseberries is the best – hard, green and full of flavour.'

250 g gooseberries, topped and tailed
70 g fructose or to taste; if you can't get fructose, use 100 g sugar
1 vanilla pod
150 ml double cream
150 ml Turkish or Greek yogurt
2 capfuls of elderflower cordial

Wash the gooseberries well and put in a pan with the fructose or sugar and a splash of water. Split the vanilla pod in half, scrape out the seeds and put the pod and the seeds into the pan with the gooseberries. Cover the pan and cook very gently for 10–15 minutes until the gooseberries have softened and broken down. Add more sugar if needed. Allow to cool completely. Whip the cream with a teaspoon of fructose/sugar into soft peaks. Stir in the yogurt and the elderflower and then gently fold in the gooseberry compôte. Spoon into individual glasses (champagne saucers are ideal) and cool in the fridge for at least 2 hours. Serve with biscuits and glasses of Muscat.

Sheep's-milk yogurt mousse with sorrel ice and nougatine

SERVES 4

This is one of René Redzepi's Michelin-starred puddings served at Noma in Copenhagen.

for the ice
500 ml still mineral water
125 g caster sugar
juice of one lemon
3 handfuls of sorrel leaves

for the mousse
150 g sheep's-milk yogurt
2 gelatine sheets, soaked
2 large egg whites
40 g caster sugar
125 ml whipping cream (in 'soft peaks')

for the nougatine
60 g icing sugar
40 g glucose powder
1 tablespoon butter
small pinch of salt
½ teaspoon green aniseed (in Denmark the seeds of a wild herb called 'sødskærm' are used but fennel would be a good alternative)

To make the ice: blend all the ingredients together in a food processor and then strain through a mouli-légumes. Freeze until hard. Using a fork, scrape the frozen sorrel into crystals, then freeze again. This can be done a day or two in advance.

To make the mousse: warm the yogurt and stir in the gelatine. Cool to room temperature. Whip the egg whites stiff, fold in the sugar and whip again. Fold the cream into the yogurt, then the egg white mixture. Spoon into a piping bag and let it set in the fridge for about 3 hours. (Alternatively, set in a bowl and spoon on to a plate before serving.)

To make the nougatine: put all the ingredients in a pan except the aniseed and heat until it boils. Cook for a minute or two (it should not take on any colour) then pour on to a baking sheet or paper. It should spread out thinly. Sprinkle with the aniseed or crushed fennel seed and let it harden. Break into four pieces.

To serve: pipe out or spoon the mousse on to four plates. Cover with the nougatine sheets. Put the ice next to it.

Summer fruits with goat's curd and East End honey

SERVES 4

Mark Hix uses East End honey for this summery pudding. 'The hives are near Romford. The bees collect nectar from the side of the railway line. It's nice, the fact that people who live in London are making honey.'

500–600 g mixed seasonal berries
150–200 g goat's curd (soft goat's cheese can be substituted)
4–6 tablespoons East End honey, or clear honey

Mix the fruits, hulling the strawberries as necessary. Spoon the goat's curd on top and drizzle generously with honey.

Summer pudding

SERVES 6–8

**900 g red and black berries, including
redcurrants, raspberries, blackberries,
strawberries and even blueberries**

175–225 g caster sugar, depending on taste

1 loaf of stale white bread

Mix the fruit and sugar together in a bowl (leave
to marinate if you have time). Put into a large pan
and cook gently for 5–10 minutes to soften the
fruit. There should be quite a lot of juice. Cut the
bread into even slices about 1 cm thick, removing
the crusts, and use the slices to line the bottom and
sides of a 2 pint bowl. Make sure there are no gaps.
Pour in half the fruit, top with a layer of bread and
pour in the rest of the fruit. Cover with another
layer of bread, trimming it so that it fits tightly. Put
a plate on top, add a couple of weights or tins to
weigh it down and leave overnight in the fridge
or larder. To serve, remove the plate, run a knife
round the inside of the basin between the bread
and the bowl, put a serving dish upside down on
top and turn the whole thing over fast. The pudding
should slide intact out of the bowl, presenting a
round and lusciously deep pink dome. If the juice
hasn't quite penetrated the bread, boil up a little of
any remaining fruit and pour over. Serve with thick
cream.

Baked peaches with ricotta

SERVES 4

A simple dish in which the peaches are infused
with lavender. Allow three peach halves per
person.

6 peaches

225 g fresh ricotta cheese

2 tablespoons caster sugar

lavender honey

fresh lavender

Preheat the grill. Halve the peaches and remove the
stones. Spoon 2 tablespoons of the ricotta into the
peach cavities and sprinkle with caster sugar. Place
under the hot grill until the sugar caramelises. Blend
the remaining ricotta with the lavender honey and
drizzle over the peaches. Garnish with sprigs of
fresh lavender.

Fig and almond tart with honey sauce by Rose Prince

SERVES 10

A final drenching of this summer tart with a hot honey and lemon sauce, and you have a rich and sticky pudding that equals any toffee sponge.

240 g unsalted butter
240 g golden caster sugar
240 g ground almonds
3 eggs, lightly beaten
5 green or black figs, quartered (peeled if the skin is tough)
for the sweet pastry
60 g icing sugar
270 g plain flour
135 g softened unsalted butter
1 large egg yolk
1–1¼ tablespoons double cream
for the honey sauce
40 g honey
juice of 2 lemons
2 capfuls of mead (optional)

You can make sweet pastry using a light, cool touch with your fingers, but it is quicker and even better made in a food processor. Put the icing sugar, flour and a pinch of salt in the processor and whizz for a few seconds. Add the butter with the egg yolk and enough cream to form a paste when the mixture is whizzed briefly. Do not overwork the paste. Remove from the processor, place on a well-floured board and lightly work into a ball, then roll to about 5 cm thick. The pastry will be very soft. Lift it by wrapping it around the rolling pin, then use it to line a 28 cm tart tin. Don't worry if it tears; just patch it with spare pieces of pastry. Chill for half an hour.

Preheat the oven to 200°C/Gas Mark 6. Prick the base of the pastry randomly with a fork, cover with greaseproof paper and fill with dry rice or beans to prevent bubbling up. Bake for about 15–20 minutes, until the edges are crisp and the base dry. You may want to lift away the paper and beans for the last 5 minutes of cooking so the base can dry out. Remove the pastry case from the oven and leave to cool. Meanwhile, make the frangipane. Melt the butter and sugar together over a low heat, stirring with a spoon or whisk, then cook for 2–3 minutes, until the mixture has a golden fudge consistency. Remove from the heat, add the ground almonds and the beaten eggs and stir until well combined. Turn the oven down to 190°C/Gas Mark 5. Pour the almond mixture into the case, then drop the fig quarters on to it, spacing them evenly. Bake for 15–20 minutes, until the frangipane is just firm and slightly puffed. Warm the honey with the lemon and mead and pour over the tart as you serve.

Elderflower fritters

SERVES 4

These delicate and flowery fritters were made in the kitchens at Belvoir castle where they harvest the elderflowers for cordials. Make the batter for the fritters just before you cook them, and eat them hot.

8 elderflower heads, each with 1 cm of stalk
120 g self-raising flour
carbonated water
sunflower oil, for frying
to serve
icing sugar
crème fraîche

Shake each elderflower head to remove any insects. Sift the flour into a bowl and add enough water, mixing until you have a batter the texture of single cream. Heat approximately 1 cm depth of sunflower oil in a pan until it sizzles when a drop of water is dropped in at arm's length. Working quickly, hold the stalk of a flower head, and dip it into and then out of the batter. Lower it into the hot oil and fry until light golden. Remove from the pan, drain on kitchen paper, and dust with icing sugar. Eat immediately, with a little crème fraîche.

Raspberry and pine kernel tart
by John Burton Race

SERVES 4

This is like a French Bakewell tart. The contrast between the soft raspberries and crunchy pine kernels works really well.

unsalted butter for greasing
plain flour for dusting
200 g sweet shortcrust pastry
for the filling
100 g ground almonds
100 g caster sugar
100 g unsalted butter, diced
3 large eggs, beaten
3 dessertspoons dark rum
100 g raspberries
100 g pine kernels

Grease a 20 cm flan tin with butter, then dust with flour. Roll out the pastry and use to line the tin. Refrigerate until needed. Place the almonds and sugar in a bowl and add the diced butter. Beat the mixture until smooth, then gradually add the eggs and rum. Preheat the oven to 200°C/Gas Mark 6 and fill the tart base with the almond mixture. Sprinkle the raspberries and kernels over the top, pushing them down. Bake for 30 minutes. Allow to cool and serve with vanilla ice-cream.

Baked stuffed peaches

SERVES 4

Succulent peaches with a rich nut stuffing and a hint of lemon.

| 2 large ripe organic peaches |
| 2 nectarines |
| 6 dried deglet noor dates |
| chopped mixed nuts to the same weight as the six dates |
| 1 egg white |
| lemon verbena, to taste |
| sunflower seeds |

Halve and stone the peaches and nectarines. Skin the dates if tough. Blend the dates in a food processor with the nuts, egg white and lemon verbena until just blended. Spoon this stuffing into the peaches and nectarines. Place in an ovenproof dish with a few tablespoons of water. Scatter with sunflower seeds and bake in a hot oven (200°C/ Gas Mark 6) for 10–12 minutes. Serve with goat's cheese or crème fraîche.

Cherry clafoutis by Raymond Blanc

SERVES 4

| 500 g ripe cherries, best quality, stoned |
| 170 g caster sugar |
| 4 tablespoons kirsch (optional, or even more!) |
| melted butter for greasing |
| 4 medium-size, organic, free-range eggs |
| 6 drops of vanilla essence (optional) |
| zest of 1 lemon, finely grated |
| 200 g plain flour |
| 100 ml milk |
| 150 ml whipping cream |
| 70 g unsalted butter |

Marinate the cherries with 2 tablespoons of the caster sugar and the kirsch for 2 hours to maximise their flavour. Preheat the oven to 180°C/Gas Mark 4. Brush the inside of a round cast-iron or china baking dish (5 cm deep × 20 cm wide) with melted butter. Add 3 tablespoons of the caster sugar and shake the dish so as to coat the inside. In a bowl whisk the eggs, the rest of the caster sugar, vanilla and lemon zest together until creamy. Add the flour and two pinches of sea salt and whisk until smooth then slowly incorporate the milk and cream. In a small saucepan heat the butter until it reaches a blonde hazelnut colour and whisk it into the mixture. Mix the batter with the cherries and their juices and pour into the baking dish. Dot with butter and bake in the preheated oven for 30–35 minutes. The clafoutis is cooked when the blade of a knife inserted into the mixture comes out completely clean. To serve, sprinkle caster sugar over. Apricots, pears or apples can be used instead of cherries.

Afternoon Tea
Traditional scones

MAKES 10 SCONES

Paul Gaylor, head chef at the Lanesborough Hotel in London, has a recipe for traditional scones to serve with clotted cream.

225 g plain flour
2 teaspoons baking powder
pinch of salt
40 g unsalted butter
25 g caster sugar
1 large egg, lightly beaten
100 ml full-cream milk, plus a little for glazing

Sift the flour, baking powder and salt together into a bowl. Rub in the butter until the mixture resembles coarse breadcrumbs, then stir in the sugar. Add the egg and the milk, then lightly mix together to form a soft dough. Roll out the dough on a lightly floured surface to 4 cm thick. Using a 6 cm cookie cutter, cut out 10 rounds, re-rolling the dough as necessary. Place the scones on a lightly greased baking sheet and brush the top with a little milk. Leave to stand at room temperature while you preheat the oven to 220°C/Gas Mark 7. Bake the scones for 12–15 minutes, or until golden. Cool on a wire rack and eat while still warm with clotted cream and strawberry jam.

St John caraway seed cake

MAKES TWO CAKES

Fergus Henderson's elevenses 'consists of a chunk of seed cake accompanied by a glass of madeira... the madeira gives a quick jolt, a bit like a firework display.' His passion for seed cake was born when a friend brought one to Tiree, the Hebridean island where the Hendersons take their summer holiday. 'Discretion with the caraway is vital. Only one pinch per cake is required. The point about seed cake is that it is good fresh from the oven when it's butttery and eggy… but it's also good when it's a day old.'

250 g butter
250 g caster sugar
5 eggs, beaten
350 g self-raising flour, sifted
2 pinches caraway seeds
milk

Preheat the oven to 170°C/Gas Mark 3. Cream the butter and sugar. Add the beaten eggs and mix until combined. Add the flour and mix until combined. Add the caraway seeds and stir until evenly distributed. Stir in a splash of milk until the mixture is of a dropping consistency. Pour into two paper-lined loaf tins and bake for 40–45 minutes, until a skewer comes out clean.

Lavender Trust cupcakes

MAKES 12

These are the cupcakes invented by Nigella Lawson to support the Lavender Trust, a charity set up in memory of the writer, Ruth Picardie, to help young women who contract breast cancer.

This recipe uses lavender sugar, made by cutting up lavender sprigs and putting them in a jar of caster sugar for a few days. Lavender sugar is also sold in supermarkets and specialist food shops. For a website address to buy it online see page 204; look here also for contact details to buy the violet food-colouring paste – grape violet – available from Jane Asher. These cakes look wonderfully fresh and summery.

for the cupcakes

125 g self-raising flour

125 g very soft unsalted butter

125 g lavender sugar, sieved

2 eggs

pinch of salt

few tablespoons of milk

for the icing

250 g Instant Royal icing powder

violet food-colouring paste

handful of lavender stalks

Preheat the oven to 200°C/Gas Mark 6 and line a 12-bun cupcake or muffin tin with paper cases. Take the butter, eggs and milk out of the fridge early so they're at room temperature. Put all the cupcake ingredients, except the milk, into a food processor fitted with a double-bladed knife, and blitz till totally combined. Process again, adding enough milk to make a batter with a smooth, flowing texture, then spoon and scrape the batter equally into the cupcake cases. Remember the cakes will rise: there is enough mixture, even if you panic when you first look at it. Bake for about 20 minutes, by which time the sponge should be cooked through and springy to the touch. Remove from the oven, leave for 5 minutes or so, then put the cupcakes in their paper cases on a wire rack to cool. Once they're cool, you can do the icing. You want it to sit thickly on the cupcakes, not run off them, and you can aid this by cutting off any risen humps with a sharp knife first so that each cake is flat-topped. Be careful not to let any crumbs besmirch the smooth topping. Make the icing following packet instructions, dyeing it a faint lilac with a spot or two of food colouring. Go carefully: we want pastel serenity here, not 1970s record-sleeve murk. Top each pretty-pale cupcake with a little sprig of lavender before the icing is set dry.

Old-fashioned lemonade
by Amy Willcock

20 organic lemons

5 litres water

670 g unrefined caster sugar (or to taste)

Peel the lemons with a potato peeler, leaving behind as much of the white pith as possible. Put the peels into a large pot and add the water. Bring to the boil. Put the juice of the lemons and the sugar into a large heatproof container and stir to combine. Pour the boiling water on to the lemon juice and sugar and stir until it is dissolved. Strain out the lemon peel. Cool and serve chilled with lots of ice.

Autumn

(SEPTEMBER, OCTOBER, NOVEMBER)

'The autumn always gets me badly, as it breaks into colours.
I want to go south, where there is no autumn, where the cold
doesn't crouch over one like a snow-leopard waiting to pounce.
The heart of the North is dead, and the fingers of cold are
corpse fingers.'

D. H. Lawrence 1885–1930: letter to J. Middleton Murry, 3 October 1924

D. H. Lawrence had a jaundiced view of the season of mists and mellow
fruitfulness. He went to Mexico to stave off the gloom, but most of us stick it
out in the brownish damp and drizzle of a typically British autumn. There are
culinary compensations of course: oysters, game and blackberry and apple pie,
mushroom hunting and the sudden blaze of colour afforded by piles of squash
and pumpkins outside the few greengrocers that remain. Now is the time to
start thinking of stews again, hot soup, root vegetables and the first frosts.
Mark Hix, Mary Contini, Nigel Slater, Antonio Carluccio and Sam and Sam
Clark tell you how...

Soups
Mushroom and potato soup

SERVES 4

Mary Contini, proprietor of Valvona & Crolla, the famous Italian deli and restaurant in Edinburgh, and Professor Roy Watling, Scotland's leading fungi expert, run autumnal mushroom-hunting days. Lunch is included and Mushroom and potato soup is often on the menu. Contini says: 'If you have fresh porcini do use them. Chanterelles are good too – or try this with chestnut or Paris brown mushrooms. Dried mushrooms can be used too.'

125 g unsalted butter

2 shallots, peeled and finely chopped

2 sticks celery, very finely chopped

2 medium-size potatoes (Maris Piper or other floury variety), peeled and grated

1.5 litres hot water

300–400 g fresh mushrooms, sliced

250 ml single cream (optional – if you use delicate fungi such as chanterelle, the cream will not be necessary)

fennel fronds from the stem, or finely choppped flatleaf parsley

Melt the butter in a pan and cook the shallots and celery until they are soft and translucent. Add the potatoes and hot water and cook for 10 minutes. Now add the sliced mushrooms and simmer the soup for 20 minutes or so. Reserve a spoonful of whole mushrooms and then taste and blend the soup. With rich fungi such as porcini the soup will be very thick – adjust the consistency with cream or hot water. Add the herbs, garnish with the reserved mushrooms and serve hot.

Spiced pumpkin soup

SERVES 4–6

Jill Norman was Elizabeth David's editor before becoming a cookery writer. This recipe is taken from her book, *Winter Food*. The smell while it's cooking is spectacular.

2 tablespoons sunflower oil

4 teaspoons ground coriander

4 teaspoons ground fennel seeds

1 teaspoon turmeric

1 large onion, chopped

2 cm ginger, chopped

2 cloves of garlic, chopped

1 kg pumpkin, peeled and cubed

2 dried chillies

2 stalks of lemongrass, bruised

600 ml vegetable stock

400 ml coconut milk

lime juice (optional)

Heat the oil in a large heavy pan and fry the coriander, fennel and turmeric until their aromas are released. Stir in the onion, ginger and garlic and fry for 3–4 minutes more, then add the pumpkin, chillies and lemongrass. Stir well, season with a little salt and add the stock. Cover the pan, simmer until the pumpkin softens, then stir in the coconut milk. Do not cover the pan now or the coconut milk might curdle. Bring the soup back to a simmer and cook until the pumpkin is soft enough to crush with a wooden spoon. Discard the chillies and lemon grass and blend the soup. Taste and, if you wish to sharpen the flavour, stir in a little lime juice. Sieve the soup and serve with bread.

Tomato, chestnut and chorizo soup

SERVES 6

The designer Jane Cumberbatch lives part of the year in Andalucia where her husband grows chestnuts. 'Chestnuts are a nutritious and useful soup ingredient, lending bulk, texture and their subtle nutty taste. This recipe is very simple to throw together and is a welcome excuse to use the tomatoes that I freeze each summer. The smoky flavour of the chorizo gives a robustness to the vegetable elements in this soup, and I would strongly advise using a decent whole-sausage chorizo for better flavour and texture.'

4 kg tomatoes, fresh, frozen or canned

2 tablespoons olive oil

1 onion, chopped

3 cloves of garlic, chopped

200 g peeled chestnuts, roughly chopped

1 litre chicken stock

100 g chorizo (the sausage-shaped one from a deli, not the thin, prepacked slices), chopped into small pieces

handful chopped parsley

Blanch the tomatoes in boiling water for one minute, remove the skins and chop roughly. Heat the olive oil in a heavy-bottomed pan and add the onion and garlic. Fry gently until limp. Then add the tomatoes and simmer for 5 minutes. Next add the chopped chestnuts and simmer for a further 3 minutes. Pour in the stock and liquidise or purée in batches. Return the soup to the pan, add the chorizo and simmer for a few minutes. Serve with chopped parsley.

Leek and potato soup with poached oysters and toast by Rose Prince

SERVES 4

Very rich, but very, very good. If you are feeling generous, use more oysters. Put the soup through a food mill (mouli-légumes) or sieve after liquidising for a velvety texture.

60 g butter

3 medium leeks, washed and chopped

1 clove of garlic, chopped

2 medium potatoes, peeled and cut into dice

600 ml chicken or vegetable stock

600 ml whole milk

150 ml double cream

salt and freshly ground black pepper

for the toast

2 slices sourdough bread

a little melted butter

4 oysters

Melt the butter in a pan and add the leeks and garlic. Cook until soft (do not let them brown), then add the potatoes. Add the stock and the milk and bring to the boil. Turn down to a simmer and cook until the potatoes are soft. Put in a liquidiser with the cream and blitz until very smooth. Meanwhile, prepare the bread. Cut into four pieces and brush on both sides with melted butter. Bake or toast until golden. Open the oysters, holding them cup side down in a cloth in your hand and piercing the pointed end with an oyster knife. Place an oyster on each piece of toast. Reheat the soup and taste for seasoning. Serve the soup in bowls, the oyster on its toast floating in the centre and a little black pepper ground on to the top.

Jerusalem artichoke and herb soup

SERVES 4

This is an adaptation of a soup by Mark Hix found in his book British.

25–50 g butter

olive oil

1 onion, chopped

1 leek, trimmed and chopped

a handful of herbs (rosemary, sage, a bay leaf, chives or thyme)

500 g Jerusalem artichokes, peeled

5 or 6 peppercorns

750 ml stock

750 ml milk

double cream (optional)

Melt the butter and heat a dash of olive oil in a saucepan, add the onion, leek and the herbs and cook until the vegetables are soft. Add the artichokes, peppercorns, most of the stock and the milk. Season with salt. Bring to the boil and then leave to simmer until the artichokes are tender (20–25 minutes). Pour the soup into a blender, adding the rest of the stock if necessary to make a smooth, creamy-looking soup. Pour into a pan, add the cream if using and reheat gently. Don't boil. Season to taste.

Duck and celery soup
by Rose Prince

SERVES 4

1 large duck carcass, or 4 mallard carcasses

little butter or dripping

2 celery sticks, roughly chopped

2 onions, roughly chopped

2 juniper berries, crushed

to serve

4 tablespoons sherry

1 celery stick

8 wild mushrooms, thinly sliced

Preheat the oven to 200°C/Gas Mark 6. Rub the carcasses with a little butter or dripping and roast until golden. Transfer to a large pan, add the vegetables and juniper berries and cover with water. Bring to the boil, skimming off any foam, then turn down to a simmer and cook for 1–2 hours. Strain the stock and pass through a fine sieve. Skim off any remaining fat.

To serve: pour the stock into a clean pan, add the sherry and bring almost to boiling point. Slice the celery stick very thinly across the stem. Add to the soup with the mushrooms. Season to taste.

Starters and Light Lunches
Fresh porcini with olive oil and lemon

SERVES 4

The gorgeous and affable Antonio Carluccio's recipe for porcini with olive oil and lemon is a classic. Simple and delicious. When porcini are out of season this dish is very good made with button mushrooms. If you want to gild the lily, add some Parmesan shavings.

500 g fresh porcini (ceps)
about 4 tablespoons single estate extra-virgin olive oil
juice of half a lemon
Maldon sea salt
leaves from 3 sprigs of flatleaf parsley, chopped

When you buy porcini, inspect them to make sure there are no maggots. You will see the holes eaten into their skin. Slice them very thinly and spread them on a plate. Stir together the olive oil and lemon juice to make a vinaigrette, then use a pastry brush to paint it on to the porcini. Season with Maldon sea salt, and scatter the parsley on top.

Celery heart and wild mushroom savoury baked custard

SERVES 2 AS A MAIN COURSE, 4 AS A STARTER

A custard of egg yolks and single cream, poured over the cooked, quartered hearts of celery and seasonal wild fungi.

2 heads of green celery, cut 10 cm from the base then quartered lengthways
30 g butter
150 g wild mushrooms (girolles or chanterelles in autumn; morels in spring), wiped clean, any dirt brushed away, or 60 g dried ceps/porcini, reconstituted in hot water and drained
2 egg yolks
90 ml single cream or half whole milk, half cream
60 g Gruyère cheese, grated

Preheat the oven to 200°C/Gas Mark 6. Bring a pan of water to the boil and add the celery hearts. Cook for about 10 minutes, or until soft. Drain on a cloth to remove as much water as possible then put into one large or several individual gratin dishes. Melt the butter in a pan and add the mushrooms. Toss in the butter until they begin to soften, then add to the celery. Mix the egg yolks and cream, seasoning with Maldon sea salt and freshly ground black pepper. Scatter the cheese over the celery and mushrooms, then pour the custard over the top. Bake in the oven until the surface is brown and bubbling (about 20–30 minutes). Serve immediately.

Caramelised cep and thyme tartlets

SERVES 4

This recipe was devised by Carolyn Robb, the Prince of Wales' chef.

300 g puff pastry (for ease and speed you can buy the pastry)
150 g shallots, sliced
1 clove of garlic, crushed
1 tablespoon olive oil
25 ml dry white wine
25 ml double cream or crème fraîche
1 teaspoon soft brown sugar
200 g fresh ceps, cleaned and quartered
50 ml olive oil
4 fresh thyme sprigs
50 g Parmesan cheese shavings

Roll the pastry out to a thickness of 3 mm, and cut it into four equal-sided triangles. Lay them out on a baking tray lined with baking parchment and chill for 20 minutes. Using a fork, prick holes in the pastry, cover with another sheet of baking parchment and lay another flat baking tray on top. Bake at 200°C/Gas Mark 6 for 8–12 minutes, until lightly golden. Remove the top baking tray and the paper and cook for 2–3 minutes more to crisp up the pastry. Cook the shallots and garlic in the olive oil until they are soft and starting to colour. Add the wine, cream and sugar and season lightly. Cook gently for 20 minutes to reduce the liquid. Cool before puréeing the mixture in a blender. Test the seasoning. Set to one side. Sauté the ceps in olive oil over a high heat to give them a good golden colour. (They are quite meaty and need to be well cooked to soften them.) Season well. Spread the creamed shallots on to each pastry triangle. Arrange the ceps on top, sprinkle with fresh thyme leaves and lay the Parmesan shavings over the top. Bake at 200°C/Gas Mark 6 for 5 minutes, then serve immediately.

Pear, Parmesan and truffle salad

SERVES 8

This is a terrifically sophisticated first course. It was created by Thierry Boué, husband of Marcia Kilgore, who founded the Bliss spa chain in London and New York. Raspberry vincotto and truffles or truffle paste are available from specialist Italian shops.

4–5 ripe Comice or Asian pears
120 g piece of Parmesan cheese
2 tablespoons raspberry vincotto
1 white Alba truffle or black Melanosporum truffle, about 25 g in weight, or a small jar of truffle paste

To avoid the pears discolouring, make this dish shortly before serving. Peel, core and slice the pears as thinly as possible and lay about five or six slices (roughly half a pear) fanned out on eight individual salad plates. Thinly shave the Parmesan on top of the pears and drizzle with the raspberry vincotto. Season with a little freshly ground black pepper, take the plates to the table, then shave the truffle thinly over each plate in front of the assembled guests. They will then have the benefit of the freshly released truffle fragrance.

Sweet potato latkes with poached egg, smoked salmon and smoked paprika crème fraîche

SERVES 4

A recipe devised by Serena Bass, New York's most famous caterer and renowned for her over-the-top parties for Hollywood A-listers such as Julia Roberts and Sarah Jessica Parker.

for the latkes (one per person)

450 g or 1 large sweet potato, peeled

225 g or 1 medium-size potato, peeled

225 g or 1 medium-size yellow onion

6 extra large eggs

40 g flour

2 teaspoons chilli powder

1 tablespoon salt

vegetable oil for frying

smoked salmon, to suit

for the smoked paprika crème fraîche

250 ml crème fraîche

4 teaspoons smoked paprika

2 tablespoons snipped chives

4 teaspoons salt

Set a pan of water over a low heat for the poached eggs. Put a large ovenproof dish in an oven heated to 150°C/Gas Mark 2. Grate the raw potatoes on the large holes of a grater. Dice the onion and add to the potatoes with two of the eggs, the flour, chilli and salt. Mix well and let rest while you assemble the crème fraîche. Mix all the crème fraîche ingredients together and set aside. In a heavy pan, over a medium flame, heat 1 teaspoon of oil per latke. Form rough cakes – don't worry if they are a little straggly – and fry for 3 minutes on the first side. Then turn down the heat, flip the latke and

cook for another 4 minutes. Cook until golden. Put them in the oven to keep warm. Poach the four remaining eggs in simmering salted water. Some people add vinegar to hold the whites together but if you use fresh eggs you won't need to. (If you are cooking for a crowd, slip the cooked eggs into a dish of warm water and cover. They won't cook any more and will stay perfect for up to 20 minutes.) Lift them out with a slotted spoon and rest the spoon on a paper towel for a few seconds to drain off the moisture. Put the salmon on the latke, the egg on the salmon and a dollop of crème fraîche on the egg. Scatter with snipped chives and compose yourself to accept accolades gracefully.

Carpaccio of grouse

Clarissa Dickson Wright's recipe for grouse carpaccio makes a brilliant starter, so long as you remember to freeze the grouse well in advance.

1 grouse breast per person
olive oil
lemon juice
cream of horseradish
1 jar of capers

Wrap the grouse breasts in cling film and freeze for 40 minutes to 1 hour. Remove them from the freezer, unwrap and slice as thinly as possible with a very sharp knife. Arrange the slices on a dish, scatter with salt and pepper, pour over some good olive oil and lemon juice and leave to stand for 10 minutes. Dot with horseradish and garnish with capers.

Spaghettini with Scottish chanterelles

SERVES 4

A useful way to use up the results of a mushroom-hunting expedition.

200 g chanterelle mushrooms
360 g spaghettini
5–6 tablespoons extra-virgin olive oil
1 clove of garlic, peeled and finely chopped
1 smallish piece of peperoncino (dried chilli), crushed
2 tablespoons flatleaf parsley, chopped

Pick over the chanterelles, trimming the bases of the stems and wiping any oil or moss away with a damp paper towel. Don't be tempted to wash them. Cut very large ones into pieces but leave the rest whole. Put the pasta on to cook in a large pan of boiling salted water. Warm the olive oil in a large frying pan. Add the chopped garlic and chilli and cook gently to flavour the oil. Raise the heat a little and add the chanterelles. They release quite a lot of moisture but don't worry – this reduces to make a natural sauce for the pasta. Toss the mushrooms in the flavoured oil for a couple of minutes. Don't overcook as they can become rubbery. Season with salt and add the chopped parsley. Take the pasta straight from the pan, letting it drain only momentarily. Toss with the sauce until well coated. Serve piping hot in warmed bowls.

Tagliatelli con funghi e pancetta

SERVES 4

15 g dried porcini, soaked in warm water

2 tablespoons extra-virgin olive oil

40 g butter

100 g smoked pancetta, chopped

200 g porcini mushrooms, cleaned and sliced

small carton of double cream

160 g egg tagliatelli

Parmesan cheese, grated

Drain the dried mushrooms through a sieve lined with kitchen towel and keep the liquid. Rinse and chop the mushrooms. Warm the olive oil and butter in a saucepan and sauté the pancetta. Add all the mushrooms and cook until they are softened. Add the soaking water from the dried porcini. Season, remembering the pancetta is quite salty. Add a small carton of double cream and warm through. Cook the tagliatelli until al dente. Strain and toss it in the sauce. Add Parmesan and serve.

Pigeon salad with figs, chickpeas and pomegranate molasses

SERVES 4

The two Sams (Sam and Sam Clark) cooked this at author Chris Stewart's house in Spain.

4 large pigeon breasts

3 tablespoons olive oil

4 figs, skins on, cleaned and cut into quarters

4 handfuls watercress or a mixture of other leaves

200 g drained, cooked chickpeas, warm

for the marinade

1 clove of garlic, crushed to a paste with salt

1 teaspoon ground cinnamon

1 dessertspoon water

1 tablespoon olive oil

for the dressing

1 tablespoon lemon juice

4 tablespoons pomegranate molasses (available in Middle Eastern food shops and delis)

3 tablespoons olive oil

Mix the marinade ingredients together, rub over the pigeon and leave for up to six hours. When you are ready to serve the salad, place a large frying pan over a medium heat, add two tablespoons of olive oil and, when hot, the pigeon breasts. Fry for 2–3 minutes on one side, then turn over and continue to fry for a further 3 minutes or until slightly pink and juicy. Remove the pigeon from the pan and set aside to rest. Meanwhile, add one more tablespoon of olive oil and, when hot, the fig quarters, and fry until slightly soft and jammy. Dress the watercress, check the seasoning and toss with the chickpeas. Spread on a large plate followed by the figs and sliced pigeon and any juice.

Cheddar and tarragon soufflé

SERVES 8

Gallery owner Detmar Blow thinks his passion
for excellent food stems from a childhood
of feast or famine (occasionally the children
would resort to eating dog biscuits to keep
going). This recipe for Cheddar and tarragon
soufflé reflects his family's love of cheese. 'We
are a family of big cheese eaters,' says Detmar.
'Mountains of it can be found in the fridge.'

25 g unsalted butter
25 g flour
900 ml whole milk
150 g unpasturised cheddar, grated
bunch of tarragon, chopped
pinch of nutmeg
8 egg whites
2 egg yolks

Make a cheese sauce by melting the butter and
then adding the flour. Stir gently to form a paste.
Slowly add the milk and whisk until it turns into a
thick béchamel consistency. Cook slowly for 10–15
minutes, add the cheese, tarragon and nutmeg,
season to taste and let the mixture cool for an
hour. When cool, beat the egg whites by hand to
a soft peak. Add the yolks to the cheese sauce
and gently incorporate the whites, stirring in one
direction with a wooden spoon. Fill individual
ramekins with the mixture, spreading evenly. Place
in a pre-heated oven at 180°C/Gas Mark 4, keeping
the oven shut for a minimum of 25 minutes. Serve
immediately.

Basmati pilaf with dill and cardamom (sooay ka pulao)

SERVES 4–6

500 ml basmati rice
3 tablespoons corn, peanut or olive oil
1 stick cinnamon
5 cardamom pods
2 bay leaves
75 g onions, peeled and cut into half rings
4 sprigs fresh dill, finely chopped
650 ml chicken stock

Wash the rice in a bowl in several changes of water.
Drain and add fresh water to cover. Leave to soak
for 30 minutes. Drain. Put the oil in a large, heavy
pan and set on a medium heat. When hot, add the
cinnamon stick, cardamom and bay leaves. Stir for
5 seconds and add the onions. Fry until they turn
reddish brown. Add the rice and dill. Turn the heat
to medium low and stir until the rice grains are
translucent (2 minutes). Add the stock and about a
teaspoon of salt if the stock is unsalted. Bring to a
boil. Cover, turn the heat to low and cook the pilaf
for 25 minutes.

Fish and Shellfish
Cromesquis d'huîtres (fried oysters)
serves 4

32 fresh oysters
100 g white flour
3 egg yolks, beaten
200 g coarse breadcrumbs
vegetable oil for frying
500 ml crème fraîche, beaten until airy
a handful of fresh basil leaves, roughly chopped
8 handfuls of mixed salad greens

Preheat the oven to 140°C/Gas Mark 1. Place a metal baking pan filled with 2.5 cm of water on the bottom rack of the oven. Open the oysters, and lay them in their shells on a baking sheet. Poach in the oven until opaque (10–12 minutes). Cool, detach the oysters from their shells, pat dry and dredge in flour, then egg yolks and breadcrumbs. Heat 7.5 cm of oil in a medium saucepan until hot. Fry the oysters in small batches until crisp and golden. Drain on paper towels. Combine the crème fraîche and basil. Serve the oysters with the salad and crème fraîche.

Smoked haddock and prawn pie
SERVES 8

Everyone loves fish pie. There's something about the fluffy, cheesy potatoes, juicy seafood and creamy chive-speckled sauce that make it irresistible. It's a perfect autumn supper that's easier to make than you think.

2 kg floury potatoes, such as Maris Piper or King Edward, peeled and cubed
1 litre milk
750 g smoked haddock fillets
100 g butter
75 g plain flour
100 g Cheddar, grated
300 ml soured cream
150 g frozen peas, thawed
400 g peeled raw tiger prawns, thawed if frozen
20 g chives, snipped

Cook the potatoes in a large pan of boiling salted water for 15–20 minutes until tender. Meanwhile, pour the milk into a sauté pan and add the smoked haddock. Bring gently to the boil, then remove from the heat and leave to stand for 5 minutes. Using a slotted spoon, transfer the smoked haddock to a plate and set aside. Measure out 200 ml of the milk for the mash; the rest will be used in the sauce. To make the sauce, melt 75 g of the butter in a heavy-based pan. Stir in the flour and cook for one minute. Gradually whisk in the milk for the sauce. Bring to the boil, stirring, then simmer gently for 3–4 minutes. Preheat the oven to 200°C/Gas Mark 6. Meanwhile, drain the potatoes and mash. Stir in the milk reserved for the mash, the remaining butter, cheese and seasoning. Then stir the soured cream and peas into the sauce together with the prawns and heat gently for a couple of minutes without boiling. Pour into a deep ovenproof dish. Stir in the chives. Flake in the haddock, discarding any skin, and season to taste. Spoon the mash over the top and rough up the surface, using a fork. Place the dish on a baking sheet and bake for 30 minutes until bubbling around the edges and golden brown.

Hake flavoured with garlic,

browned with fresh herbs and caramelised tomatoes

SERVES 4

4 thick, 200 g steaks of hake
50 ml olive oil
4 cloves of garlic, unpeeled
herbs to garnish
for the caramelised tomatoes
5 tomatoes on the vine
30 ml olive oil
a pinch of caster sugar
1 clove of garlic, finely sliced
10 basil leaves, chopped
for the herb butter
100 g fresh white bread, crusts removed
200 g softened butter
15 g parsley leaves, chopped
2¬3 tarragon sprigs, chopped
2–3 chervil sprigs, chopped
2–3 basil leaves, chopped
2 shallots, finely chopped

To make the caramelised tomatoes, preheat the oven to 110°C/Gas Mark ¼. Peel the tomatoes, cut them in half and deseed them. Put them in an ovenproof dish and coat them with the olive oil. Sprinkle with pepper, sugar, garlic, salt and basil. Bake in the oven for about 90 minutes until they are caramelised and bubbling. To make the herb butter, put the bread in a low oven (120°C/Gas Mark ½) and bake until it breaks up easily into small dry crumbs (about 30 minutes or so). Put the crumbs into a bowl and add the butter, herbs and shallots, season with salt and pepper and mix well together. Spread the herb butter out on a flat baking tray (about 3 mm thick) and put in the fridge to solidify. When it is hard enough, cut it into four rectangles, similar to the size of the fish steaks. To cook the hake, cover each steak with a rectangle of the butter mixture. In a pan, heat the olive oil and gently fry the garlic cloves. Peel the cloves, cut each one into four and insert them into the butter on the hake steaks. Preheat the oven to 180°C/Gas Mark 4. Season the steaks, put them on a large, flat ovenproof dish with a sprinkling of olive oil, and place the dish in the oven for 20 minutes. When they are done, take them out and put them under a hot grill to finish browning. Garnish with herbs and serve with the tomatoes.

Oysters with spinach and saffron sauce

SERVES 4

a large pinch of saffron threads

24 oysters

120 g spinach, thick stalks removed

20 g butter

a squeeze of lemon juice

120 ml dry vermouth

100 ml double cream

1 egg yolk

Crumble the saffron threads and soak in 2–3 tablespoons of hot water. Open the oysters, making sure to sever the oyster from the muscle that attaches it to the shell. Reserve the deep shells and strain the liquor into a bowl. (You don't need it for this dish, but it is too good to waste. Freeze it and use in a fish soup.) Blanch the spinach leaves, drain well and chop. Melt the butter in a frying pan and cook the spinach gently for a few minutes. Season with pepper and lemon juice. Sprinkle a good layer of coarse salt on to a grill or baking tray for the oysters to sit in. Put a little spinach and an oyster into each shell and place them on the salt. Meanwhile heat the vermouth and saffron water in a small pan and reduce by half. Whisk the cream and egg yolk together lightly and pour into the vermouth. Cook gently, without boiling, until the sauce thickens enough to coat the oysters. Heat the grill. Spoon the sauce over the oysters and put them under the grill for 1–2 minutes to brown the surface lightly. Serve at once.

Smoked eel risotto

SERVES 4

Unlike fresh eels, smoked eel is widely available.

2 tablespoons olive oil

1 large onion, finely chopped

100 g Arborio risotto rice

50 ml white wine

500 ml vegetable or chicken stock

20 g butter

25 g diced smoked eel

20 g grated Parmesan

8 thin slices smoked eel

In a large saucepan heat the oil and then add the onions and cook until very soft. Stir in the rice. Add the wine and stir until evaporated. Add about a fifth of the stock and stir until it has been absorbed by the rice. Repeat this process with the remainder of stock or until the rice is cooked but al dente. Stir in the butter and diced eel and season. Add the Parmesan and stir. Serve the risotto in bowls garnished with slices of smoked eel.

Meat, Poultry and Game
Steak

SERVES 1

Gordon Ramsay says, 'When I'm at home, the last thing that I want to do is spend hours in the kitchen. With this in mind I tend to keep the food I cook at home as simple as possible, although I still insist that it tastes good. One of my favourites is a nice piece of sirloin steak. I have the most amazing butcher near me called Randall's and his beef is among the best you'll find in London.'

---

1 sirloin steak

half a head of garlic

butter

a sprig of thyme flowers

'I simply rub the meat all over with half a head of garlic and pan-fry it in lots of foaming butter with a few thyme flowers. I like my sirloin medium–rare as cooking it slightly longer crisps up the fat, but it is still nice and tender. To go with this I make a salad with whatever is in the fridge. Usually this consists of rocket, watercress, chopped spring onion, apple and avocado, bound with a light classic vinaigrette. That's enough for me as I make a lot of salad, but if I have some crusty bread at hand, then I'll use that to mop up all the juices.'

Confit of lamb with butternut squash purée and cassoulet of haricot beans and red onions

SERVES 4

Don't be put off by the rather overwhelming amount of oil in this recipe – the result is meltingly tender.

---

1 litre extra-virgin olive oil

1.3 kg fresh shoulder of lamb, boned, rolled and tied

250 g dried white haricot beans

2 large tablespoons unsalted butter

1 carrot, diced

3 red onions, finely chopped

3 sprigs of thyme

1 clove of garlic, chopped

1 butternut squash, peeled, seeded and diced

Preheat the oven to 190°C/Gas Mark 5. Heat the olive oil in a large iron casserole or Le Creuset – over the hob – keeping it just below smoking point. Season the lamb shoulder with salt and freshly ground pepper, lower it gently into the casserole and then cook in the oven for 2 hours. Fast-boil the haricot beans for 20 minutes, then turn down to a simmer for a further 30–45 minutes – they should be tender but not mushy. Melt half the butter in a separate pan and add the carrot, onions, thyme and garlic. Stir in the haricot beans with about two ladles of the cooking liquid and cook gently for a further 15 minutes. Meanwhile bring the squash to the boil in a pan and cook until tender, then mash with the rest of the butter. Season with salt. Remove the lamb from the oil, slice and serve with the squash purée and cassoulet beside it.

Devilled lamb's kidneys

SERVES 4-6

Great for breakfast or brunch and delicious on toast for supper. Kidneys are one of the most versatile cuts available.

12 lamb's kidneys, halved and trimmed of sinews
cayenne pepper
2 tablespoons oil
15 g butter
2–3 shallots, peeled and chopped
100 ml dry white wine, or sherry if preferred
2 teaspoons mustard
2 teaspoons tomato purée
150 ml chicken stock
cream
1 tablespoon anchovy sauce
half a bunch of flatleaf parsley, finely chopped

Season the kidneys with cayenne and a little salt. Heat the oil in a frying pan and fry the kidneys for 2 minutes on each side until they are firm. Transfer to a plate. Melt the butter in the pan, add the shallots and cook for a couple of minutes. Add the wine, the mustard and the tomato purée and simmer for a minute or two. Add the stock and simmer until the sauce thickens. Add a dash of cream and the anchovy sauce, season and stir. Return the kidneys to the pan. Simmer for a minute to reheat, scatter on the parsley and serve with boiled rice or on toast.

Saddle of fallow deer with anchovies

SERVES 6–8

1 saddle of fallow deer
2 tins of anchovy fillets
50 g lard or pork fat for barding
3 onions, sliced
lard or olive oil for frying
300 ml red wine

Preheat the oven to 220°C/Gas Mark 7. With a sharp pointed knife make incisions all over the meat and put an anchovy fillet in each. Season with pepper. Cover the meat with the barding fat and secure it with skewers. In a heavy oven dish fry the onions in the lard until coloured. Place the meat on the onions, add salt and pour over the wine. Roast for 15 minutes to seal the meat, and then reduce the heat to 170°C/Gas Mark 3, allowing a cooking time of 15 minutes per 450 g.

Crackling pork

SERVES 8–10

Richard Vaughan farms free-range pigs in the Wye valley and supplies pork to chefs such as Fergus Henderson, Rowley Leigh and Bruce Poole.

2 kg pork leg, loin or belly (ask the butcher to remove any hairs and score the skin)

2 large pinches soft crystal sea salt

olive oil

Preheat the oven to 180 °C/Gas Mark 4. Place the pork in a large colander in the kitchen sink and pour boiling water over it to open the scoring on the skin. This will help the cooking of the crackling. Rub the skin with the salt; do not use more than the recommended amount or the pork will be uneatable. Rub the underside of the meat, avoiding the skin, with the olive oil and place on a rack in a roasting dish and then put into the oven. Cook the pork for 2 hours, more for a heavier joint, then remove from the oven. If the crackling is not yet crisp, cut it away from the meat and return it to the oven for 15 minutes. Slice the pork and the crackling and eat hot with potatoes and tomatoes roasted in pork fat and salsa di mele (apple and onion sauce), or cold with parsley, black olive and anchovy sauce.

Mutton slow-roasted with woody herbs, meadow hay and butter, served with gravy

SERVES 12

Several years ago the Prince of Wales fired the starter pistol in the mutton 'renaissance'. Speaking during a muttony dinner for farmers, butchers and chefs held at the Ritz, he relayed the virtues of reviving a taste for the meat of sheep that are one year old or more. He reminded all present how, without the mutton on the hillsides of Britain, the landscape we all love to walk about on would be lost. The Weatheralls, who farm sheep in Lanarkshire, supply some of London's more resourceful chefs – Fergus Henderson of St John, Mark Hix of the Ivy and Rowley Leigh, now of Café Anglais. 'The five-year-old Blackface ewe spends four years on the hill. The meat takes its flavour from the heather and blaeberries, but the finishing on the grass puts on extra meat and fat,' says Ben Weatherall. 'Then you just have to hang the meat properly, as we do, for two weeks.' The Weatheralls always eat their own five-year-old Blackface mutton. Silvy Weatherall wraps it in foil with an insulating pillow of woody herbs and meadow hay, then roasts it slowly for about three hours. She puts it on the table among her own feather sculptures; the tanned leg lying among an array of giddy high heels decorated with the plumes of birds, some of which may have lived on the same hill as the mutton.

All mutton needs gentle cooking in order to retain the juices and tenderness in the meat. Mutton that has been roasted slowly overnight in a simmering oven (Agas are ideal for this method) has a beautiful melting texture but the 3-hour roast in the following recipe suits the Blackface meat perfectly. The idea of wrapping the mutton in hay or herbs is an old one. It both flavours the meat but, more importantly, insulates it so that the joint cooks at an even low temperature. It is essential that meat cooked this way is 'rested' in a warm place for at least half an hour after cooking so that the juices settle back into the meat. When you open up the foil at the end of the cooking the smell is heavenly.

375 g unsalted butter, softened
fresh ground black pepper
cloves from 3 heads of garlic, peeled and crushed
4 sprigs of rosemary
1 bunch of fresh thyme
a few sprigs each of marjoram and oregano, or a few lavender stalks
1 leg of mutton (approximately 3.5 kg), the hock bone severed so that it fits in a roasting pan
4 handfuls of hay (the pet shop will provide if you have no other supply)
'lamb' stock for gravy – made by roasting a few lamb or mutton bones (available from the butcher) until coloured then braising them in 1 litre water with onion, carrot and celery for about 1– 1½ hours
2 tablespoons capers, chopped (optional)

Preheat the oven to 230°C/Gas Mark 8. Combine the butter with about three pinches of freshly ground black pepper and the garlic. Chop half the herbs finely and add to the butter mixture before slathering all of it on to the joint. Line a roasting pan with aluminium foil, then make a bed of half the hay and half the remaining herbs. Lay the mutton on top then cover with the rest of the hay and herbs. Bring the foil around and pinch it together to seal. Bake in the oven for about 2.½ hours – a large leg may need 20 minutes more – then remove from the oven and leave to rest in a warm place for about 30 minutes. Lift from the pan and keep warm, sieve the juices in the pan and set aside. Pick out any stray pieces of stalk and hay from the pan and set over the heat. Add about 600 ml of stock and bring to the boil. Simmer for a few minutes and pour into a warm jug. (Capers go well with mutton; add to the gravy in the final stages if desired.) Serve with slices of the roasted mutton and vegetables.

Overnight-baked mutton

SERVES 12

A simmering oven in an Aga is ideal for this recipe – switch other ovens to a low, 100°C/ Gas Mark ½ setting. Be a little vigilant the first time you attempt this in case your oven thermostat is not 100 per cent reliable.

120 g butter, softened
1 leg of mutton (approximately 3.5 kg)
fresh ground black pepper

Spread the butter on to the surface of the leg, season with black pepper, put it in a roasting pan, cover with foil and put in the oven. If you intend to eat the mutton for lunch at 1 pm, put it in at 9–10 pm the previous night. About 1½ hours before serving, take it out of the oven, drain off the juices and fat, reserving the juices for gravy, and put the mutton in a hot oven (220°C/Gas Mark 7) for one hour. Let it rest after roasting for 20 minutes in a warm place, then serve.

Lancashire hotpot

SERVES 4

1 tablespoon butter, melted

600 g large new potatoes, peeled and sliced thickly

3 medium-size onions, chopped

2 tablespoons dripping

1 sprig of thyme

16 middle-neck salt-marsh lamb chops

4 lamb kidneys, quartered, the ducts trimmed off

1 heaped tablespoon plain flour

20 ml Worcestershire sauce

500 ml lamb stock

4 medium-size carrots, sliced

100 g samphire or 4 strips of anchovy

Preheat the oven to 170°C/Gas Mark 3. Butter the base of a casserole and spread a single layer of potatoes over it. In another pan, sauté the onions in the dripping with the thyme until transparent. Set aside. Dust the lamb and kidneys with the flour and fry on both sides briefly in the dripping – also set aside. Add the Worcestershire sauce to the hot pan and stir, scraping the bits from the bottom. Add the stock and bring to the boil. Layer the meat, with the carrots, some potatoes, bay leaves and either samphire or anchovies in the casserole. Pour over the stock and finish with a layer of potato. Put the casserole in the oven and bake covered for 3 hours. Remove the lid, turn up the heat and bake for 20 minutes to finish browning the potatoes. Rest for 20 minutes before serving.

Grouse with honey toast
by Rose Prince

SERVES 2

Painted with honey, the first grouse of the season is served on toast, crisped in the oven, then spread with a little more of the nectar.

2 grouse, plucked and oven ready

2 tablespoons butter

4 pinches of sea salt

4 pinches of freshly ground black pepper

2 slices of white or wholemeal bread

4 tablespoons honey

to serve

2 handfuls of chard leaves

2 teaspoons walnut oil

2 teaspoons balsamic vinegar

Preheat the oven to 190°C/Gas Mark 5. Put the grouse in a roasting pan and insert a teaspoon of butter and some salt and pepper into the cavity. Rub some softened butter into the breast. Spread more butter on to both sides of the bread and place on a separate tray. Roast the grouse for 35 minutes. After 20 minutes, put the bread in the oven and bake until golden and crisp (it should be ready at about the same time as the grouse). Heat the honey in a small pan. Paint the honey on to the surface of the grouse and return to the oven. Cook for a further 5 minutes then leave in a warm place for 15 minutes to allow the juices to work their way back to the centre. Carve off the breasts and twist off the legs. To serve, dress the chard leaves with the walnut oil and balsamic vinegar and divide between two plates. Spread each piece of crisp toast with a thin layer of honey, place each on the leaves and balance the grouse on top.

Partridge with cabbage

SERVES 4

An excellent way to use old birds. Allow half a partridge per person.

1 Savoy cabbage, cut into quarters

2 partridge

75 g butter

1 carrot, chopped

1 onion, chopped

1 thick piece of bacon

4–6 chipolata sausages

bouquet garni of parsley, thyme and a bay leaf

a glass of red wine (optional)

225–300 ml stock

Heat a pan of water and boil the cabbage quarters until tender. Meanwhile, put the partridges into a flameproof casserole (large enough to take both them and the cabbage). Add the butter, carrot, onion and bacon, season and flame over a medium heat. Add the chipolatas and brown slightly. Put in the bouquet garni, add a dash of wine if using and pour on the stock. Allow to bubble for 20 minutes and then add the cabbage. Add a little more liquid if necessary. Cover and cook until the birds are done (a good hour). To serve, take out the cabbage and arrange on a serving dish, halve the partridges and lay on top of the cabbage with the sausages. Pour over the sauce.

Potée champenoise

SERVES 12, OR 8 IF YOU HAVE SPENT THE MORNING GRAPE-PICKING

Perfect for a harvest lunch in Champagne.

1 kg haricots blancs (dried or tinned)

1 large free-range chicken

8–12 smoked sausages

2 pork tongues

1 kg pork belly

2 pork hocks

sprig of thyme

2 bay leaves

sprig of rosemary

1 white cabbage (cut into 8 or more equal pieces from stalk to top)

16 small carrots

16 small potatoes

1 large turnip, diced

parsley to garnish

If you are using dried beans, these need to be pre-prepared according to the manufacturer's instructions. Joint the chicken and put the meat and the sausages in a large covered saucepan of water with the herbs and salt and pepper. Cook on a low heat on the hob for at least an hour until the meat is tender. Remove the meat, keep warm in a separate dish and put all the vegetables, including the beans, into the stock and cook on a low heat for about half an hour, or until the vegetables are tender, adding extra water if necessary. Return the meat to the pan and heat through. Spoon into large soup bowls and garnish with parsley. Serve with gherkins, small white onions and moutarde de Meaux or Dijon mustard on the side.

Pheasant in the Georgian style
with pomegranate

SERVES 4–5

This is a recipe that has descended through the ages, each generation adding or taking away an ingredient as they felt necessary.

30 walnuts, or 225 g shelled

900 g grapes

1 green teabag

1 pheasant

flesh from 4 pomegranates, squeezed through a muslin or sieve to produce the juice

120 ml sweet muscatel wine, e.g. Frontignan

olive oil

For perfect results pour boiling water over the walnuts, leave for a few minutes, then skin. If you find this impossibly fiddly, don't worry. Preheat the oven to 180–190°C/Gas Mark 4–5. Liquidise and sieve the grapes to obtain a thick juice. Pour 120 ml of boiling water over the teabag, brew for 5 minutes, then strain off the tea and reserve. Put all these ingredients, with the pheasant, the pomegranate juice, the wine and a tablespoon of olive oil, into a casserole. Ideally this should be only a little larger than the bird so the liquid almost covers it. Season. Bake in the oven for 50 minutes or until the pheasant is just cooked. Carve, put on a serving dish, surround with the strained walnuts and keep hot in the oven while you boil down the cooking juices. You should end up with 350–470 ml. Pour over the pheasant and serve either on its own or with rice or bulgar wheat. If you prefer to cook the fractionally less healthy version, substitute four blood oranges for the pomegranates, butter for the olive oil and thicken the sauce with butter and flour.

Pan-roasted duck legs and potatoes by Rose Prince

SERVES 2

This is a quick way to cook a roast without using the oven; it is only possible with a heavy cast-iron casserole with a well-fitting lid. The legs are a cheaper way to enjoy duck, as butchers are always preoccupied with selling the breast meat. As the legs cook they release their fat, the perfect roasting medium for the potatoes.

2 duck legs

soft crystal sea salt

3 medium-size potatoes, peeled and cut in half

juice of half a lemon

sourdough bread

a punnet of cress

2 tablespoons cornichons (pickled baby cucumbers)

Prick the duck legs with a skewer, sprinkle with the salt and put them in the pan with the skin side down. Cook over a low heat until they release some fat. Turn up the heat and cook for about 5 minutes, until they are brown. Add the potatoes, stir to get a coating of fat, and cook over a medium heat, covered for 15 minutes then uncovered for another 35 minutes. Occasionally turn the potatoes and meat so that every surface browns. Squeeze the lemon juice over the duck before serving with the bread. Put a bowl of cress and cornichons beside each plate.

Vegetables
Scallion champ

Darina Allen's scallion champ is perfect cold-weather fare. This recipe appears on the menu at Ballymaloe House in County Cork.

1.3 kg unpeeled old potatoes, e.g. Golden Wonders or Kerrs Pinks
110 g chopped scallions or spring onions (use the bulb and the green stem)
350 ml milk
55–110 g butter

Scrub the potatoes and boil them in their jackets. Finely chop the scallions or spring onions. Cover with cold milk and bring slowly to the boil. Simmer for about 3–4 minutes, turn off the heat and leave to infuse. Peel and mash the freshly boiled potatoes and, while hot, mix with the boiling milk and onions. Beat in some of the butter. Season to taste with salt and freshly ground pepper. Serve in one large or four individual bowls with a knob of butter melting in the centre.

Colcannon

SERVES 4–6

The traditional Irish dish – this is Myrtle Allen's version.

6–8 potatoes
1 head of cabbage
about 14 cups of milk
50–110 g butter

Scrub the potatoes and put to boil in salted water. Quarter, core and finely shred the cabbage. Put in a very little boiling water and boil rapidly, turning occasionally until cooked and all the water has evaporated. Peel the potatoes and mash with milk. Stir in the cabbage immediately and beat very well. Taste for seasoning. Serve in a warm dish, hollowing the centre a little. The butter is placed in the hollow to melt slowly into the vegetables.

Risotto aux cèpes

SERVES 10

Paul Old is a winemaker based in France. This improvised recipe comes from two of his friends, vineyard owners from Melbourne who come over to Europe every autumn for the picking season. It was devised especially to match Hugo Stewart and Paul Old's Terret wine, a pale, dry white made from the oldest and rarest grapes they cultivate.

50 g dried ceps (or any kind of dried mushrooms)

250 g butter (to taste)

white wine

250 g field mushrooms (or Portobello mushrooms), finely chopped

100 g oyster mushrooms, finely chopped

6 cloves of garlic, minced

3 leeks, finely chopped

1.5 kg risotto rice

2 cubes of vegetable stock in 2 litres of boiling water, with white wine to taste (1–2 glasses)

300 g Parmesan, grated

flatleaf parsley, to garnish

Put the dried ceps in just enough water to cover them and soak for 10 minutes. Drain, reserving the jus. Gently sauté the ceps in half the butter, adding a splash of white wine and the reserved jus. Keeping this mix on a low heat, add the rest of the mushrooms. You can add more butter to taste at this stage. Cook this mushroom mixture for 5–10 minutes and then set aside until it is needed. In a separate (large) pan, cook the garlic and leeks in the rest of the butter until they start to change colour. Now add the rice and continue cooking until the rice turns translucent. Add the vegetable stock and white wine mix, cover and cook for about 30 minutes, checking occasionally (you should not need to stir repeatedly) that it is not sticking to the bottom of the pan. In the last 15 minutes add the mushroom mix. Just before serving add the Parmesan and flatleaf parsley.

Swiss chard and potatoes

SERVES 4

500 g potatoes, peeled and cut into large pieces

1 kg chard, large stalks removed and leaves cut into 5 cm ribbons

4 tablespoons olive oil

3 cloves of garlic, chopped

Boil the potatoes in a large pan of salted water for 10 minutes until about half cooked. Add the chard to the potatoes, bring to the boil and cook until the chard is tender (3–4 minutes). Drain, reserving some of the cooking water. Heat the oil in another large pan and sauté the garlic lightly. Add the potatoes and chard and season with salt and pepper. Stir to coat the vegetables with the oil. Add a ladle or two of the cooking liquid, crush some of the potato into it to thicken slightly, and cook until the vegetables are in a light sauce. Serve with grilled lamb or fish.

Roast potatoes

SERVES 4–6

This is Nigel Slater's excellent recipe for roast potatoes.

---

about 5 large, floury potatoes

lard, dripping or fat from the roast

Peel the potatoes. Cut them into a comfortable size (you alone know how big you like your roast potatoes to be). Put them in a saucepan of cold water and bring them to the boil. Add salt, half a teaspoon or so, then turn them down to an enthusiastic simmer. Give them a good 5 minutes, maybe a bit longer, until they are slightly soft around the edges. Drain the water off and return the pan to the heat. Shake the pan so that the edges of the potatoes are slightly scuffed. This will give them wonderfully crisp edges once they are roasted. Tip them into a shallow metal pan in which you have heated the fat – you just need a shallow pool of it in the bottom of the tin – then roll the spuds in the fat and roast in a preheated oven at 200°C/Gas Mark 6 until thoroughly golden and crisp. They will need a good 45 minutes. Move them only once or twice during cooking, otherwise the edges will not brown and crisp. Tip off any extra fat, sprinkle the potatoes with salt and return to the oven for a few minutes longer until they are truly crisp.

Pan-roast tomatoes with garlic and thyme

SERVES 4

This was cooked on an outdoor fire by the charcoal burners of East Sussex. Alastair Hendy, photographer, chef and travel writer says: 'With each breath of wind, there's a pinging tinkling sound as the coals catch... the oil lamps sigh. We roasted herbed and garlic rubbed quail, flat field mushrooms and roast tomatoes... and ember-roast whole garlic, which we squeeze from its husks on to just baked flat bread.'

---

3 cloves of garlic, sliced

1 small bunch of thyme, stalks removed

5 tablespoons olive oil

1 loaf of crusty bread

1 large punnet of cherry tomatoes

For easy transportation to the barbecue site, mix the sliced garlic and thyme leaves with the olive oil and add a few good twists of black pepper and some salt. Put this in a small container. Slice the bread and wrap in a bag or foil, and pack the tomatoes in their punnet. At the fire or barbecue, set a frying-pan over some very hot embers with two tablespoons of the garlic and herb oil and fry the cherry tomatoes until their skins begin to split. Meanwhile, stick some sliced bread on a stick or toasting fork and get someone to toast it over the fire as you fry up more of the oil to spill over the wood-fired bread. Spoon the fried tomatoes, garlic and thyme over the toast, along with the glorious juices, and tuck in.

Lancashire cauliflower cheese

SERVES 4

Peter Ascroft grows cauliflowers on the silt plains near Preston. The area is famous for its cauliflowers as well as celery and lettuce. His family have farmed here for more than 100 years. 'My dad was a cauliflower grower and both my grandfathers... All I have ever been into is farming. I have been driving tractors since I was five. I plant more than a million cauliflowers a year...' This recipe for cauliflower cheese uses up just one of them...

800 g cauliflower, broken into florets

350 ml milk

1 pinch of grated nutmeg

1 bay leaf

1 heaped tablespoon butter

1 heaped tablespoon plain flour

60 g Lancashire cheese, cut into 1 cm pieces

30 g Gabriel cheese or Parmesan, grated

Blanch the cauliflower florets in boiling water for two minutes and drain. Refresh with cold water. Heat the milk to boiling point with the nutmeg and bay leaf. In another pan melt the butter, add the flour and cook until the texture becomes sandy. Add the hot milk in a steady stream, whisking. Continue to whisk until the mixture boils and thickens. Season with salt to taste and add the Lancashire cheese. Fold in the cauliflower and transfer to a gratin dish. Scatter the grated cheese on top and bake until golden on top.

Baked potatoes with Gruyère and onion

SERVES 4

1 kg linzer or similar potatoes, scrubbed clean and cut into walnut-sized cubes

60 g unsalted butter

extra-virgin olive oil

1 large, firm onion, diced

2 teaspoons chopped fresh thyme

200 g oak-smoked back bacon in one piece, cut into chunks

220 g Gruyère cheese, grated

2 tablespoons crème fraîche

fleur de sel

Preheat the oven to 180°C/Gas Mark 4. Bring the potatoes up to the boil in salted water and drain. In a non-stick sauté pan heat half the butter with a little olive oil until foaming. Add the onion and potatoes and fry over a medium-high heat until golden. Season and add half the thyme. Remove with a slotted spoon to a terracotta dish. Add the remaining butter to the pan and fry the bacon until crisp. Add the remaining thyme and scatter over the potatoes, mixing together gently. Sprinkle with the Gruyère and dot with the crème fraîche. Sprinkle with freshly ground black pepper and fleur de sel, and bake in the oven for 10–12 minutes or until golden. Serve straight from the oven with crusty bread and a salad of bitter leaves tossed with mustard, olive oil, salt and pepper.

Sliced potatoes in tian with sage

SERVES 4

8–10 potatoes, finely sliced

4 cloves of garlic, mashed

small handful of fresh sage leaves

600 ml full-cream milk

Preheat the oven to 180°C/Gas Mark 4. Lay the sliced potatoes in a buttered baking tray, sprinkle with the garlic and sage, add salt and pepper, and mix together well. Pour the milk on the mix and bake for one hour.

Baked butternut, delicata or sweet dumpling squash

The thin line that separates a summer squash from a winter squash corresponds, according to Alan Davidson the food writer, 'to differences in use... rather than divisions between the botanical species'. Winter squashes mature on the vine and can then be stored and used over winter. Their skins are hard and inedible but the flesh inside is often a better flavour than that found in summer squashes. And, of course, they look wonderful. One of the most heartening sights in a gloomy autumn is a blazing pile of yellow, red and orange squashes, striped, flecked and twisted into weird and fantastical shapes, and bearing names as odd as their appearance: Hoka, Chirimen, Sweet Mama, Chinese Alphabet and Winter Crookneck.

I small squash per person, whichever type you fancy

2–3 tablespoons crème fraîche, depending on fruit size

I tablespoon chopped fresh sage for each squash

Parmesan cheese (optional)

With delicata and sweet dumpling squash, roast the fruits whole. With butternut squash, cut them in half lengthways and scoop out the seeds. Drizzle the cut flesh with olive oil and sprinkle with salt and pepper. Bake the squash on a baking tray for about 45 minutes at 200°C/Gas Mark 6. Prick with a fork to check that the flesh is soft. If not, give it 10 minutes more. Take the squash out of the oven and leave it to cool enough for you to handle. Scoop out most of the flesh with a spoon and, in a bowl, mix this with the crème fraîche and herbs. Spoon the mixture back into the empty skins. For a richer main course, you can sprinkle a bit of Parmesan and sage over the top and bake for 15 minutes, or until the top starts to go brown and crunchy.

Puddings
Pain perdu aux pommes

SERVES 4

Simon Hopkinson first ate this apple dessert at Marc Meneau's restaurant L'Esperance in northern Burgundy. He has adapted this recipe from Meneau's book *La Cuisine en Fêtes* – essentially, it is French toast with apples.

for the custard

250 ml milk

½ vanilla pod, split lengthways

4 egg yolks

50 g caster sugar

for the caramel sauce

50 g butter

120 g caster sugar

6 tablespoons whipping cream

2 egg yolks

for the apples

4 Granny Smith apples, peeled, halved, cored and cut into wedges

60 g butter

4 thick slices of good baguette (a touch stale, if possible), cut on the diagonal

First make the custard. Scald the milk with the vanilla pod in a heavy-bottomed saucepan and leave to infuse for 10 minutes. Remove the pod, rinse, dry and store in a jar of caster sugar, so flavouring the sugar for further confections. Briefly beat together the egg yolks and sugar and then strain the hot milk over them, whisking as you go. Return to the saucepan and cook over a very low heat (with a heat-diffuser pad if possible) until limpid and lightly thickened. When you think it is about ready, give a final vigorous whisk and pour into a bowl. Cover and cool. Note: if you split the custard, a blast in a liquidiser will rescue it. Make the caramel sauce by melting the butter with half the sugar in a small pan until golden brown. Add half the whipping cream (it will splutter slightly) and stir together until well amalgamated; it should be the colour of butterscotch. Keep warm. Mix the egg yolks with the remaining sugar and whipping cream in a shallow soup plate, or similar. Set aside. Lightly colour the apples in 30 g of the butter using a small frying pan, but do not cook through. Transfer to the caramel sauce and finish cooking them in this until tender. Keep warm. Melt the remaining butter in a large frying pan, briefly soak the bread slices in the egg yolk/sugar/cream mixture and then fry over a fairly high heat until golden on both sides and puffed up. Drain on kitchen paper. To assemble, place one piece of bread on each plate, arrange the apples along their length, spoon over the caramel sauce and finally dribble some of the custard all around the bread.

Baked Johanna Gold apples with currants and cognac, sweet cream and fresh nutmeg

SERVES 10

10 Johanna Gold apples (you can substitute
Gala or Cortland cooking apples)

200 g sugar, for baking, more for dusting

90 g currants or raisins

zest of 1 lemon

zest of 1 lime

zest of 1 orange

125 ml cognac, plus more for cream

125 ml cider

110 g butter, cut into 2.5 cm cubes

nutmeg

cinnamon

double cream

Preheat the oven to 190°C/Gas Mark 5. Slice the bottoms off the apples and core; spread evenly in a buttered baking dish. Mix the sugar, currants, fruit zest, cognac and cider together and pour the mixture into each holed apple. Pour the remaining mixture over all the apples. Dot the apples with the butter. Grate some fresh nutmeg and cinnamon over all the apples, sprinkle with some more sugar and bake until soft (about 45 minutes). Beat 2–3 cups of double cream until just whipped, add a touch of cognac and serve with the apples.

Spiced syllabub

SERVES 8

This recipe needs to be started a day in advance.

250 ml decent red wine

1 stick of cinnamon

8 cloves

90 g caster sugar

rind of 1 unwaxed orange or 2 unwaxed
tangerines

rind of 1 unwaxed lemon

300 ml double cream

sprigs of rosemary or crystallised rose petals,
to decorate

Put all the ingredients except the cream and rosemary into a pan and bring slowly to the boil. Pour into a bowl, cover and leave to infuse for 12–24 hours. Strain into a large bowl and add the cream slowly, stirring all the time. Whisk until the mixture thickens and holds a soft peak on the whisk. It will take several minutes. Spoon into glasses and refrigerate or put in a cool place until needed. Put a small sprig of rosemary or a few crystallised rose petals on the top of each one before serving.

Windfall toffee apples cooked over an open fire in East Sussex

SERVES 4

8 baby apples, such as small Coxes or 16 cultivated crab apples

juice of a lemon mixed with water

500 g light muscovado sugar

100 g butter

2 sticks of cinnamon, broken in half

250 ml double or whipping cream

2 tablespoons rum

Peel the apples and put in a bowl of acidulated (lemon-juiced) water, to prevent browning. Put the sugar and 1 tablespoon of water in a small saucepan and stir over a gentle heat until the sugar has melted, then allow it to build enough heat to turn deep gold and caramelise. Stir in the butter, watching out for hot splutters. Drain the apples and pack with the cinnamon into a deep dish or tin and pour over the toffee caramel. Cover loosely with foil and bake in an oven at 180°C/Gas Mark 4 for 45 minutes or until the fruit is tender. (Alternatively you can do this in a covered saucepan on the fire, but watch that it doesn't catch and burn.) Whip the cream with the rum into soft peaks. Serve the apples with some of their toffee sauce on pillows of soft whipped rum cream.

Apple and blueberry crumble

The superseed, hemp, a mild relation of grass, is used in this recipe for apple and blueberry crumble. It's accompanied by cider custard.

700 g apples, peeled, cored and chopped into small chunks

300 g blueberries

1 tablespoon dark brown sugar

for the crumble

175 g self-raising flour

75 g cold butter, cubed

110 g dark brown sugar

100 g hempseed

for the cider custard

2 egg yolks

200 ml cider

2 tablespoons muscovado sugar

1 tablespoon cornflour

4 teaspoons cinnamon

400 ml cream

Pre-heat the oven to 200°C/Gas Mark 6. Mix the apples with the blueberries and the sugar in a large baking dish. Sieve the flour into a large mixing bowl then rub the butter into the flour until it looks like coarse sand. Mix in the sugar. (If you have a food processor you can just drop in the butter, flour and sugar and pulse till it is at sand stage.) Mix in the hempseed to make it crunchy, then spoon the crumble mix over the fruit in the baking dish, compacting it fairly firmly. Bake for 40 minutes. In a saucepan over a low heat, mix together the first five custard ingredients with a whisk until well combined. Add the cream, whisking constantly, and continue to whisk until the custard has thickened, not letting it boil.

Tarte aux raisins

SERVES 8

'The most expensive tart in the world' – made from the grapes picked at Krug Clos de Mesnil, the legendary walled vineyard owned by the Krug family. One and a half kilos make three tarts or one bottle of champagne.

for the pastry

200 g flour

100 g caster sugar

100 g butter, cut into pieces

50 ml hot water

a little extra butter and sugar for the tart tin

for the filling

500 g chardonnay grapes (muscat or English-grown white-wine grapes can also be used)

5 plain biscuits (morning coffee or digestives), crushed

75 g vanilla sugar

Preheat the oven to 180°C/Gas Mark 4. Grease a tart tin with butter, and sprinkle with sugar, pressing it lightly into the butter. This will give the base a slightly caramelised effect. Put the tin in the freezer for 30 minutes. Wash the grapes, drain and dry with kitchen paper. Sieve the flour into a mixing bowl and add the sugar, a pinch of salt and the butter. Rub the butter into the flour and sugar mixture until it resembles fine breadcrumbs. Slowly drizzle in the hot water and begin to knead into pastry. Form the pastry into a ball shape and roll out flat until it is roughly 4 mm thick. Use it to line the cold tart tin. Spread a thin layer of crushed biscuits over the base. Spread the grapes evenly over the biscuit layer and dust with the vanilla sugar. Cook in the oven for about 25 minutes.

Apple and blackberry pie

SERVES 4

60 g icing sugar

270 g plain flour

135 g softened unsalted butter

1 large egg yolk

1–1½ tablespoons double cream

1 egg beaten with milk, for eggwash

for the filling

300 g blackberries

8 apples, peeled and cored

a pinch of cinnamon

sugar to taste

caster sugar to dust

Make the pastry in a food processor, whizzing the icing sugar, flour and a pinch of salt together for a few seconds. Add the butter with the egg yolk and enough double cream to form a paste when the mixture is whizzed briefly. Do not overwork the paste. Divide into two lumps, one slightly larger. Work into flat discs and rest for 30 minutes in the fridge. Meanwhile stew the blackberries and apples in a pan until soft. Add the cinnamon and sugar to taste. Preheat the oven to 200°C/Gas Mark 6. Remove the pastry from the fridge and allow to return to nearly room temperature before rolling on a floured board. Roll into two rounds, line a 25 cm tin with the larger piece. Fill with the apple mixture. Brush the rim of the pastry with egg wash. Lay the other round on top and pinch together the edges. Brush the surface with eggwash and bake for 30 minutes or until golden. Dust with caster sugar and eat hot with cream.

Baking
Chocolate brownies

MAKES ABOUT 24 PIECES

Chantal Coady runs Rococo Chocolates in the Kings Road, London. This is her friend Mandy's recipe for fabulously fudgey brownies. 'Mandy read Italian at Bristol University (where she met my husband, James). She then married an Italian air steward and now lives in La Dolce Vita territory near Ostia Lido, outside Rome. She leads a whirlwind life, single-handedly bringing up three children, guiding groups of Americans around Rome, and making these famous brownies.'

350 g butter
140 g unsweetened cocoa powder
6 eggs
675 g caster sugar
250 g plain flour
3 teaspoon real vanilla essence
100 g shelled fresh walnuts, roughly chopped

Preheat the oven to 180°C/Gas Mark 4 and line a fairly deep baking tray, about 20 × 30 cm, with greaseproof paper. In a large, heavy pan, melt the butter with the cocoa. Whisk the eggs, then whisk in the sugar, then the flour and vanilla. Finally, add the cocoa and butter mixture and the nuts. Pour into the prepared tray and bake for 40–45 minutes, or until springy to the touch. Do not overcook, or you'll loose the fudginess. Cut into squares while warm and leave to cool.

Cheese straws

1 x 500 g packet of puff pastry
250 g cheddar cheese, grated
1 teaspoon paprika
100 g hempseed, salted
1 egg

Preheat the oven to 220°C/Gas Mark 7. Roll out the pastry into a large rectangle, about 50 × 30 cm. Mix the cheese, paprika and most of the hempseed with some black pepper in a bowl then cover half of the pastry with the mix. Fold over the other half of the pastry then roll again. Fold in half and roll out again. Fold in half one last time and roll once to seal. Crack the egg into a cup, whisk, then paint over the pastry. Sprinkle the remaining seed on top then cut into strips and place on a baking tray. Bake for about 15 minutes until puffy and golden brown.

Sweet potato bread

MAKES 3 LOAVES

1 kg strong bread flour
300 g sweet potatoes boiled until soft in their skins, peeled
25 g fresh yeast
1 tablespoon salt
500 ml warm water

Place the flour and potatoes in a large bowl and mix with your hands. Crumble in the yeast and dissolve the salt in the water. Add the water until you have workable dough with a mixture that does not stick to the sides. Pummel down with the fists. Stretch out the bottom of the dough then fold back on top and continue pummelling. Do this with the sides and top for about 10 minutes. Shape into three round loaves before leaving to prove for 14 hours. Cook in the oven at 220°C/Gas Mark 7 for about 25 minutes. Leave to cool.

Apple and walnut cake

SERVES 6

This recipe was created by Richard Allen, executive chef at Harvey Nichols in Leeds. He makes it with apples grown in the 60-year-old orchard at Ampleforth Abbey where Friar Rainer Verbog looks after 2000 trees, including romantically named varieties such as Beauty of Bath, Ribston Pippin, Wagner and Belle de Boscop.

350 g apples, Granny Smiths or Bramley
juice and zest of ½ a lemon
100 g butter
150 g sugar
1 egg
1 teaspoon vanilla extract
1 teaspoon ground cinnamon
185 g plain flour, sifted
½ teaspoon bicarbonate of soda
½ teaspoon baking powder
50 g chopped walnuts/hazelnuts
40 g sultanas, soaked in 35 ml cognac for several hours or overnight

Preheat the oven to 180°C/Gas Mark 4. Line a 15 cm cake tin with paper and set aside. Peel the apples and slice enough to arrange in the bottom of the tin. Grate the remaining apples and mix with the lemon juice and zest. Cream together the butter and sugar until pale and fluffy. Gradually add the egg and vanilla, beating after each addition. Fold in all the dry ingredients as well as the grated apples and sultanas. Pour over the arranged apple slices in the tin and level off. Bake for 40 minutes to 1 hour, reducing the temperature to 150°C/Gas Mark 2 (if the cake colours too quickly) for the last 15 minutes. A knife when inserted will come away clean when the cake is cooked. Cool in the tin for half an hour, then remove from tin to finish cooling.

Winter

'Winter is icummen in,
Lhude sing Goddamm.
Raineth drop and staineth slop,
And how the wind doth ramm!

Skiddeth bus and sloppeth us,
An ague hath my ham.
Freezeth river, turneth liver,
Damn you, sing: Goddamm.

Ezra Pound 1885–1972: 'Ancient Music' (1917)

How well Mr Pound sums it all up – the awful realisation that the ramming
wind and the sheets of slop now landing on your head are yours for the duration.
Until well into March, probably... If ague has your ham, then you want to be
somewhere warm, near a large fire with a glass of whisky in one hand and the
sound of someone else in the kitchen producing hot and comforting dishes. Like
hot-smoked salmon, chicory soup, perhaps, or winter sauce and chestnut stuffing,
pot-roast chicken, pork belly and plum puddings. In a while, the person in the
kitchen might emerge with a little dish of quail biryani to tempt you back to life.
Tom Norrington Davies, Nigel Slater, Darina Allen, Madhur Jaffrey and Raymond
Blanc help you survive until spring.

Soups
A fast, warming bowl of soup

PER PERSON

This recipe is by Nigel Slater and is taken from his book, *Appetite*.

chicken stock

2–3 small, hot red peppers, depending on your heat threshold

a couple of thick, young blades or several thinner stems of lemongrass

a small handful of Asian noodles

greens – such as spinach, mustard greens or dark, tender cabbage

Using a soup bowl as a measure, pour as much stock as you want to eat into a deep saucepan. I suggest two deep bowlfuls per person. Bring the stock to a boil. Slice the peppers very finely and remove the seeds if you wish (they carry some heat). Smash the lemongrass blades with the handle of a knife so that they splinter but stay together, then add them to the stock with the peppers. Turn the heat down and leave until the lemongrass has given up some of its flavour. Taste the stock regularly, but you can reckon on about 15 minutes. Meanwhile, cook the noodles for a minute or two in boiling water. They need a bit of bite to them. Drain them and drop them into cold water so they don't stick together. Sort through the greens, throwing out anything that isn't perky, then tear them into pieces. Fish the lemongrass from the stock, then add the greens. Taste for salt. Once the greens have softened to a velvety texture – about a minute for spinach, a bit longer for cabbage or mustard greens – divide the noodles among warm bowls and ladle over the stock, greens and peppers.

Simmered gammon with watercress dumplings in broth by Rose Prince

SERVES 4

1 kg raw gammon

2 shallots, peeled and halved

2 large carrots, sliced diagonally

1 stick celery, very thinly sliced

2 star anise

about 1.4 litres fresh beef or chicken stock

for the dumplings

60 g suet

120 g self-raising flour

leaves from 1 bunch watercress, chopped

for the watercress oil

leaves from 1 bunch watercress, chopped

4 tablespoons olive oil

Put the gammon in a pan and cover with water. Bring to the boil, then throw the water away. Add the vegetables to the pan with the star anise and cover with stock. Bring to the boil, removing any scum. Turn down the heat until simmering slowly and cook for 1½ to 2 hours until the gammon is tender. Season with black pepper. Meanwhile, mix together the suet, flour, watercress and half a teaspoon of salt. Add cold water, a tablespoon at a time, until you have a dryish dough that just holds together. Lightly shape into walnut-size rounds. Pound together the watercress and olive oil with a pinch of salt until it becomes a smooth green emulsion. Pour half the broth from the gammon into a separate pan, bring to the boil and drop the dumplings in one by one. Cook until they float to the surface and small bubbles erupt on their surface. Chop the gammon into bite-sized chunks and serve with the dumplings, vegetables, and broth. Zig-zag a little watercress oil over each plate.

Creamed chicory soup with pink pepper, parsley oil and soft boiled egg by Rose Prince

SERVES 4

A light, thin soup with an intense bittersweet chicory taste, to eat as a robust winter starter.

60 g unsalted butter

2 medium-size onions, chopped

5 chicory, roughly chopped, the inner core removed

600 ml chicken stock

600 ml whole milk

60 ml double cream (optional)

2 teaspoons red peppercorns (baie roses)

4 eggs

for the parsley oil

8 springs tender parsley, chopped

4 tablespoons olive oil

Melt the butter, add the onions and chicory and cook for about 15 minutes over a low heat until the vegetables are translucent and soft. Add the stock, milk and cream and bring to the boil. Turn down to a simmer and cook for another 10 minutes. Liquidise or blend until smooth in a food processor and season with salt. Crush the red peppercorns using a pestle and mortar or pepper grinder or put them in a strong plastic bag and bash them with a rolling pin. Prick the rounded end of each eggshell with a pin so it does not crack during cooking, put in a pan and cover with water. Bring to the boil and count 4 minutes from boiling point. Flush under cold water until you can handle them and peel, being careful to leave the egg whole. Blend the parsley, oil and some salt in a pestle and mortar or a food processor to a smooth, thick oil. (If using a food processor you may have to make more to get the right effect but parsley oil is delicious with pasta, fish and grilled meat.) Serve the soup piping hot, with the egg in the centre and a trail of parsley oil across the top. Scatter a large pinch of crushed pink pepper over each, and remember to put plenty of bread on the table.

Cocklety soup by Darina Allen

SERVES 6

4 dozen cockles

30 g butter

1 small onion, finely chopped

30 g celery, chopped

30 g flour

600 ml creamy milk

120 ml double cream

1–2 tablespoons parsley, chopped

Wash and scrub the cockles well in several changes of water to get rid of the sand and grit. Put them in a large saucepan with a tablespoon or two of water, cover and steam for 4–5 minutes until the cockles are open. Discard any that do not open. Strain the cooking liquid and set aside. As soon as they are cool enough to handle, remove the cockles from their shells, leaving two or three in their shells for each serving. Melt the butter in a saucepan. Add the onion and celery and cook over a gentle heat until soft, but not coloured. Stir in the flour, then add the strained cockle juice and milk. Cook for a minute or two, stirring all the time, until the soup is smooth and silky. Add the cream and chopped parsley, and season with salt and freshly ground pepper. Simmer gently for 10 minutes. Finally add the cockles and serve.

Fish and Shellfish
Mackerel with rhubarb and chilli

SERVES 2

Choose very shiny, firm mackerel with clear eyes. Line-caught mackerel from the sustainable south-coast fishing grounds are sold in Sainsbury's and Tesco, marked with the Marine Stewardship Council logo (MSC).

2 forced rhubarb stalks, cut into 1 cm pieces

1 tablespoon sugar

2 tablespoon lemon juice

1 mild red chilli, de-seeded and chopped

fillets from 2 fresh mackerel

Cook the rhubarb with the sugar and lemon juice until just soft. Add the chilli, stir once and leave to cool. Heat a grill pan or heavy bottomed frying-pan. Grill the mackerel on each side for about 2 minutes. You will not need fat. Serve – skin-side up for looks – with a large spoonful of the rhubarb sauce on the side and a big watercress salad.

Sitka seafood stew

SERVES 4

This seafood stew is served up at a fish restaurant in the Alaskan outpost of Sitka. Colette Nelson, who runs Ludvig's Bistro, uses local Dungeness crabs in this stew, but the meat from a British spider or brown crab (see suppliers on page 204) will be as good. Serve in large bowls, with plenty of toasted bread.

2 tablespoons olive oil

8 scallops, sliced in half

500 g white fish, cut into chunks

1 glass of white wine

600 ml fish or vegetable stock, warmed with a pinch of saffron threads

500 g cooked white crabmeat

for the reduction

2 kg tomatoes, halved and the pips removed

6 tablespoons olive oil

6 cloves of garlic, peeled, crushed to a paste with salt

1 head of fennel, chopped into small dice

1 star anise, crushed

2 tablespoons Spanish smoked paprika

1 tablespoon dried oregano

1 tablespoon red wine vinegar

1 bottle of red wine

First make the red wine and tomato reduction (this can be made well in advance). Preheat the oven to 200°C/Gas Mark 6. Brush the tomatoes with some of the oil and roast for about 45 minutes or until they begin to blacken at the edges. Remove from the oven and allow to cool. Heat the remaining oil and add the garlic and fennel. Cook until transparent and slightly soft; add the tomatoes with the spices, oregano and vinegar. Add the red wine and bring to the boil; stew for about an hour, until reduced to about a litre. Keep hot. Just before you eat, heat the last 2 tablespoons of oil in a large, preferably non-stick or very heavy-bottomed pan, until you can see white – blue vapour. Quickly add the scallops and white fish. Turn and sear on both sides, then pour in the white wine and stock. When it boils, add the crabmeat, stir briefly then ladle in the red wine and tomato reduction. Bring to the boil, add salt and pepper to taste, and serve.

Fortune's kipper paté

SERVES 2-3 PEOPLE

Barry Brown and his brother Derek are fifth-generation kipper makers in the business founded by their great-great-grandfather William Fortune in Whitby in 1872. Fortune's tiny shop and smokehouse is hidden away in a narrow cobbled street overlooking Whitby harbour. This is Barry's wife Liz's recipe for kipper paté.

1 pair of kippers

1 dessertspoon single cream

lemon juice to taste

Cut the heads and tails off the kippers, then microwave for 2½ minutes, fresh side up, or wrap the kippers in foil and bake in a hot oven (230°C/ Gas Mark 8) for 15 minutes. Save any oil formed by the cooking in a bowl. When the kippers are cool, place on a plate and remove the bones and skin, putting the flesh into the bowl with the reserved oil. Transfer to a blender, add the cream and lemon juice and blend to a thick paste. Serve with thick-cut toast. The paté should be kept refrigerated and used within 4 days.

Hot-smoked salmon with potato and leeks

SERVES 4

5 large baking potatoes, peeled (Maris Piper would be suitable)

3 large leeks with most of the tougher green tops removed, chopped

70 g butter, plus some for buttering the flan dish

1 tablespoon grain mustard

170 ml double or single cream

520 g hot-smoked salmon

freshly ground black pepper

Preheat the oven to 220°C/Gas Mark 7. Slice the potatoes into 0.5 cm discs and parboil for four minutes. Sauté the leeks in the butter until soft, then add the mustard, seasoning and the cream. Gently break up the salmon into chunks and reserve, ready for the final assembly.

Butter a 30 cm heavy flan dish and begin building up layers of potato, leek mixture and salmon pieces. The final layer should be potato. Melt the remaining butter and brush over the final potato layer. Season with a lot of black pepper. Bake until the upper surface is nicely browned (35–45 minutes) and serve with a green salad.

Meat, Poultry and Game
Pork belly with fennel, garlic and Marsala

SERVES 4–6

1 tablespoon fennel seeds, finely ground
2 cloves of garlic, crushed
1 kg pork belly, skin scored
1 tablespoon hempseed oil
150 ml Marsala

Preheat the oven to 220°C/Gas Mark 7. Mix the ground fennel seeds and the garlic to an aromatic paste and season with salt. Rub the paste under the pork belly. Place on a board, skin-side up, and dry off the skin thoroughly with a cloth or kitchen towel. Sprinkle the skin with salt. Transfer to a large roasting tray, skin-side up and drizzle with the hemp oil. Roast for 30 minutes, then reduce the heat to 190 °C/Gas Mark 5 and cook for another 1½ hours until tender. Take the pork out of the roasting tray and set aside. Pour off the excess oil, and put the roasting pan on the hob over a medium heat. Add the Marsala and reduce by a third, scraping the bottom to release the juices and flavour stuck to the tray. Strain and serve over the pork.

Remoulade with air-dried mutton

SERVES 4

The slightly hot and spicy, celery and mustard taste of remoulade salad is addictive, and perfect beside the robustly flavoured cured mutton. For suppliers of Herdwick mutton see page 204.

200 g air-dried Herdwick mutton, very thinly sliced
400 g celeriac (about half a large root), peeled
1 carrot, peeled
2 egg yolks
1 level teaspoon English mustard
90 ml extra-virgin olive oil
a few drops of white wine vinegar
45 ml Dijon mustard

Remove the mutton from the fridge one hour before you intend to serve it. Shred the celeriac and carrot with a coarse grater. Put the egg yolks and English mustard in a ceramic bowl and beat in the oil slowly and evenly with a wooden spoon. Add the white wine vinegar and a pinch of salt. Stir in the grated celeriac and carrot, and then the Dijon mustard. Arrange the mutton on four plates, serve the remoulade beside it, shake over a little more extra-virgin olive oil and finish with a twist of freshly ground black pepper.

Venison Napoleon

This dish celebrates the 'auld alliance,' says the ebullient restaurateur Ranald Macdonald who cooked it for a family Christmas in Scotland. 'It's inspired by my ancestral cousin the Duc Tarentum.' The fillet is stuffed with a duxelle of mushrooms, duck livers, haggis (see suppliers on page 204), onions and whisky. For a richer dish, marinate the fillet for up to 24 hours in red wine with no more than four crushed juniper berries, six crushed black peppercorns, a fistful of fresh thyme, loads of garlic, a good pinch of nutmeg and the juice and zest of half an orange. You can use the marinade for gravy/sauce later but strain off the ingredients to avoid bitterness.

allow the following per guest:

140 g venison fillet

50 g butter

10 g shallots, finely chopped

1 large clove of garlic, finely chopped

40 g finely chopped Scottish chanterelle mushrooms (or the best equivalent)

15 g duck liver

2 teaspoons truffle paste or 1 teaspoon black truffle oil

15 g Macsween haggis

1 tablespoon Macallan 10-year-old Fine Oak whisky

Pastry (500 g will be enough to cover 1 kg piece of venison fillet)

2–3 egg yolks, beaten

Preheat the oven to 220°C/Gas Mark 7. Season and seal the venison fillet in a very hot, heavy pan (if you have marinated it, wipe it off well before sealing very thoroughly), and put to one side. To make the duxelle, melt the butter in a pan on a gentle heat. Add the shallots, garlic and then about a minute or two later (being careful not to burn the butter or brown the shallots), the mushrooms. After a few more minutes add the rest of the ingredients in the order listed above and gently cook, continuing to stir for another couple of minutes until you have reduced the ingredients to a rich brown paste. At no point should anything burn. Season with sea salt and black pepper. When the duxelle mixture and the venison fillet have cooled, roll the pastry and cut into an oblong shape. Paste the duxelle over the pastry, place the fillet in the middle and fold the pastry over the fillet, ensuring that you gently press the pastry firmly into the meat for a nice fit. Seal the pastry connections with egg yolk on the underside, then brush all over with egg yolk. Place in the oven and remove when the pastry is a golden brown. Leave to rest in a warm place for 6–8 minutes before serving. The venison will be medium rare. Serve with spinach, mashed celeriac, roast potatoes and gravy.

Pot-roast chicken

SERVES 4

1 chicken, about 2 kg

1 medium-size onion

half a lemon

a few sprigs of thyme

2 tablespoons olive oil

100 ml white wine

a small handful of fresh parsley, chopped

Preheat the oven to 180°C/Gas Mark 4. Check that the cavity of the chicken is clear and then stuff with the onion and lemon. Tuck the sprigs of fresh thyme inside the chicken and under the wings and legs. Drizzle the olive oil over the bird and season with black pepper. Put the chicken in either a deep casserole with a lid, or a high dome-covered baking dish. Pour the white wine around the bird and cook for 45 minutes. Remove the lid, add the parsley and return to the oven for a further 20 minutes to brown the bird. Set the bird aside while you tip the juices from the pan and the chicken cavity into a small pan. Skim off any fat. Carve the bird and serve with the juices poured over the meat.

Venison with plum wine and salted plum paste by Mark Edwards

SERVES 4

The clean meat of wild venison matches well with umeboshi, Japanese salted plum paste, and Japanese plum wine (for suppliers see page 204). The paste is available from Sainsbury's.

480 g wild, culled venison meat cut into 60g pieces, sinews removed

120 g butter

60 g onions, finely chopped

2 courgettes (golden if available), chopped

200 ml plum wine (or substitute sloe gin)

30 g umeboshi (salted plum paste)

Season the venison pieces well with salt and freshly ground black pepper, sear in a hot pan (or on a griddle over hot coals) with a little oil until medium rare, and remove immediately. Melt the butter in the pan, add the chopped onions and cook for a minute until soft but not coloured. Add the courgettes to brown. Add the plum wine, and cook until the liquid has reduced by two-thirds. Stir in the plum paste and pour over the venison.

Koftas (meatball curry)

SERVES 4–6

This is a recipe by Madhur Jaffrey. Madhur Jaffrey first learnt to cook out of homesickness while studying at RADA (she went through her mother's culinary repertoire on a gas ring in her digs). Since then in a remarkable dual career that spans nearly 40 years, she has written 20 books and appeared in more than 30 films, including *Shakespeare Wallah*. 'Serve the koftas on white plates,' she says, 'I only ever eat off white plates.'

for the meatballs

450 g ground/minced lamb

4 medium-size onions, peeled and finely chopped

5 cm fresh ginger, peeled and grated

3 cloves of garlic, peeled and crushed to a pulp

1 tablespoon ground coriander

½ teaspoon ground roasted cumin seeds

4 teaspoons Kashmiri red chilli powder

3 tablespoons fresh coriander, chopped

1 egg, lightly beaten

for the sauce

5 cm fresh ginger, peeled and chopped

4–6 cloves of garlic, peeled and chopped

2 fresh, hot green chillies

4 tablespoons olive oil or other vegetable oil

2 large black cardamom pods, lightly crushed

1 teaspoon whole cumin seeds

4–6 whole cloves

5 cm stick of cinnamon

4–5 green cardamom pods

2 onions, peeled and finely chopped

4 medium-size tomatoes, grated on the coarse part of a grater, or enough to get 350 ml

4 teaspoons Kashmiri red chilli powder

4 tablespoons plain (natural) yogurt

Combine the ingredients for the meatballs, mix well and, with wetted palms, form 24 balls. Arrange in a single layer on a plate, cover and refrigerate for at least 6 hours. To make the sauce, put the ginger, garlic and green chillies, along with 3 tablespoons of water, into a blender. Blend to a smooth paste. Heat the oil in a wide, heavy pan over a medium-high heat, then add the black cardamom, cumin, cloves, cinnamon and green cardamom. Stir, then add the onions. Fry for about 8 minutes, or until the onions are reddish golden. Add the ginger paste, turn the heat down and stir for 2 minutes. Add the grated tomato and red chilli powder. Stir and cook on a medium-high heat until the tomatoes are reduced to a dark paste and you begin to see the oil. Turn the heat to medium and add the yogurt, a tablespoon at a time, until it has all blended with the sauce. Add 475 ml of water. Season and stir. Slide in the meatballs so they lie in a single layer. Cover and simmer for 50–60 minutes, shaking the pan every now and then – never stirring.

Jaggery and garam masala grilled quail with quail biryani

SERVES 8

Malini and Rahul Akerkar run Indigo, the Indian equivalent of the Ivy in London, in the Colaba district of Bombay. This is their Indian version of Christmas lunch – 'tiny Christmas birds roasted with a jaggery-based marinade (jaggery is a form of unrefined sugar made from the date palm) and arranged round lightly spiced biryani filled with moist pieces of breast meat, fresh mint and coriander'. Garam masala is a mixture of several powdered spices – cinnamon, cloves, black pepper, black and/ or green cardamom, bay leaf, fennel or star anise and sometimes cumin or coriander. Most Indian provision stores sell ready-made garam masala powder mixes that work very well. This dish requires that you marinate the quail overnight in a refrigerator, so start a day before.

Melt the jaggery over a medium heat in a heavy-bottomed pan and caramelise slightly. Add the oil and spices and cook till fragrant. Be careful not to char or burn the mixture. Remove from the heat, and add the lime or lemon and the orange juice. Mix well and let cool. Marinate the quails in the spiced jaggery mixture overnight, in a non-reactive dish in the refrigerator. Preheat the oven to 180°C/ Gas Mark 4. When you are ready to serve, remove the quails from the refrigerator and truss the birds. Reserve the marinade. Grill for a few minutes on both sides, basting often with the reserved marinade. Make sure you only sear or partially cook the birds. Transfer the quails to an ovenproof dish, pour some of the remaining marinade over them and roast in the oven for about 15–20 minutes. (You can leave the partially cooked, grilled quail in the marinade for half an hour before roasting.) Remove the birds from the oven, cut off the trussing string and serve with the quail biryani.

for the grilled quail

100 g jaggery or raw cane sugar

2 tablespoons grapeseed or other cooking oil

1 teaspoon fresh ginger paste

1 teaspoon fresh garlic paste

2 cinnamon sticks, coarsely crushed

4–5 whole cloves

1 teaspoon freshly crushed black pepper

60 ml fresh lime or lemon juice

60ml fresh orange juice

8 quail, cleaned

for the biryani

500 g onions, thinly sliced

vegetable oil for deep frying

750 g basmati rice

4–5 mace pods

4–5 bay leaves

250 g clarified butter or ghee

1 tablespoon fresh ginger paste

1 tablespoon fresh garlic paste

1 teaspoon turmeric powder

2–3 cinnamon sticks

8–10 green cardamom pods

750 g quail meat, skinned, and cut into small chunks

110 ml chicken stock

1 tablespoon cashew paste

110 ml cream

1 tablespoon garam masala powder

150 g mint leaves

300 g coriander, chopped

30 g raisins, soaked in water to rehydrate

30 g unsalted cashew nuts

Rub two-thirds of the onions with several teaspoons of salt and set aside in a colander to drain for about 1 hour. Then wash them under running water to remove the salt. Pat them dry with a paper towel. Deep fry the onions in enough oil to cover till golden and crisp and set aside to drain on a paper towel. Keep to one side until you are ready to serve the biryani. Wash the basmati rice and discard the water. Add fresh water to cover the rice and let the rice soak for 15 minutes till it plumps. Drain off the water. Separately bring water to a boil with the mace and bay leaves – you'll need about 300 ml of water and about a quarter teaspoon of salt for every 200 g of basmati rice. Add the drained basmati rice and cook for about 8–10 minutes or till the rice is cooked al dente. Don't overcook the rice as it must continue cooking in its own steam later on. You may have to add a little more hot water as necessary, but do not drown the rice. Drain off any extra liquid and reserve the rice, covered tightly with a lid. While the rice is cooking, in another pan on medium heat, sauté the remaining onions in half the clarified butter. Add the ginger and garlic pastes, turmeric, cinnamon and cardamom and cook the spices for a few minutes. Add the quail meat and cook till the meat sears. Add the chicken stock and cashew paste and continue to cook until the mixture thickens. Add the cream and reduce to a smooth gravy. Remove from the heat and set aside. In another heavy-bottomed pan, add the remaining butter and the cooked rice and sprinkle with the garam masala powder. Lightly sauté for a few minutes and then add the quail and its gravy to the rice. Add the mint, coriander, half the fried onions and drained raisins to the rice and mix to achieve an uneven incorporation of all the ingredients. You should have a fluffy, marbled white and brown rice and quail mixture. Cover the pot tightly and set on a warm stove to finish cooking in its own steam. Remove and serve hot, garnished with the remaining crispy fried onions and cashew nuts, and accompanied with the grilled quail.

Tagine of quail with dates

SERVES 4

Before you go out and buy a tagine... *make sure it will fit into your oven* and, if you are seduced into buying one while on holiday in Morocco, remember it'll probably need its own seat on the plane back home. These dishes, traditionally used by nomads as portable ovens over charcoal braziers – the base being both a cooking and serving dish – are enormous. They're also terrifically heavy and will break into a million pieces if you drop them. That said, however, they do produce stews and casseroles of matchless flavour and tenderness.

4 oven-ready quails

4 dates, pitted

pinch of saffron

2 tablespoons olive oil

1 medium-size onion, finely sliced

40 g fresh ginger, peeled and sliced

1 cinnamon stick

3 sprigs coriander, tied with string

200 ml water

Place half a date under the skin of each quail breast, then season the quails with salt, pepper and the saffron. Heat the oil in a tagine over a gas ring, and brown the quails on both sides. Add the onion, ginger, cinnamon and coriander. Cook until the onion is soft and lightly coloured, then add the water. Bring to the boil; reduce heat so that the water is just barely trembling. Cook, covered, for about 45 minutes, then cool. Remove the breasts and legs from the carcasses. Pick the spices out of the tagine and replace the meat on top of the onion. Reheat until the sauce becomes syrupy.

La poule au pot (poached chicken in winter-vegetable broth)

SERVES 4

Raymond Blanc's recipe for poached chicken in broth can be cooked a couple of hours in advance and reheated just before you need it.

1 organic, free-range chicken (about 1.6 kg), with giblets and any traces of blood removed

3 litres cold water

8 banana shallots, peeled

8 small carrots, peeled

2 medium-size turnips, peeled and cut into 8 segments

2 leeks, trimmed, washed and cut across

4 sticks of celery, washed and cut across into 8 pieces

8 cloves of garlic, peeled

1 bouquet garni (consisting of 8 sprigs of parsley, 4 sprigs of thyme, 3 bay leaves and a sprig of tarragon)

8 black peppercorns

20 g sea salt

Place the chicken in a saucepan just large enough to hold it and the vegetables. Cover with the cold water and bring to the boil. Skim, add the remaining ingredients and simmer very gently (so that the bubbles are just breaking the surface) for 40–50 minutes. To check if the chicken is cooked, pierce the thigh with the blade of a thin knife. If the liquid runs pink the chicken will require some further cooking; when the juices run clear the chicken is done. Turn off the heat and allow to rest for 20 minutes. Remove the chicken from its broth and carve into eight pieces. Serve in soup bowls with some of the vegetables and plenty of the broth.

Liver and bacon

SERVES 2

Chef Tom Norrington Davies enthuses about liver: 'Liver, bacon and onions were made for each other, but for some people this meal would be very low down on a list of good things to eat. The reason is invariably its association with school dinners. How did that come about? Was there a manual in school kitchens up and down the land called "How to Make Children Hate Liver?" Once overcooked, liver is irredeemable. It not only becomes tough and powdery, it also takes on a bitter taste. The best way to avoid spoiling the liver is to make this instead of a casserole – and it takes less time, too.'

2 tablespoons plain flour

2 generous, evenly cut slices of liver, about 1.5 cm thick (ask the butcher to do it for you)

1 tablespoon butter

4 slices smoked bacon or pancetta, cut into strips

3 or 4 sage leaves

1 medium-size onion, finely sliced

1 glass red wine

1 teaspoon tomato purée

You should serve this with mash, which you can get ready before you start on the liver. A tight-fitting lid on the pan will keep it hot. Season the flour with salt and pepper and sprinkle it over a tray or large plate. Dust the liver slices with the flour and set aside. Heat a heavy-bottomed pan or skillet and melt half the butter in it. Fry the bacon or pancetta strips until they are as done as you like them (I'm a crispy-bacon man, but each to his own). Remove them with a slotted spoon and put to one side. Leave the fat in the pan and fry the sage and onion until the sage is nicely wilted -- this should only take a couple of minutes on a high heat. If the onion catches a little, so much the better. Remove from the pan and put to one side. Now fry the liver. For pink liver, give it about 2 minutes on each side over a fairly high heat. When it is done, lift it out and plonk it straight on top of the mash. The last bit is incredibly quick and easy. Let the pan get hot again and immediately throw in the onion and the bacon. Pour in the red wine and let the whole thing bubble up. Sometimes, if the red wine is very boozy, you will get a little flambé action (it doesn't always happen and it needn't). If the alcohol doesn't burn off, it will evaporate anyway. Should you, bizarrely, be seducing someone with liver and bacon, you may want to be sure of the flames, in which case fortify the wine with a very small slug of brandy. Once the wine has bubbled up, add the tomato purée, the remaining butter, salt, pepper and, if you like, a pinch of sugar (depending on the fruitiness of the wine). Douse the liver in this gravy and tuck in.

Roast game birds by Rose Prince

SERVES 6

In late autumn the glut of pheasants reaches its peak. It's a good moment. The birds are still feeding on the supplement corn put down by farmers and there's a little yellow fat around the breasts. Partridges, which have a slightly longer season, are still around; mallard is abundant, and there are the rarer treats: woodcock, snipe and the occasional late grouse. The principles when cooking any of these birds are the same. Butter is important, pepper and salt too – but timing is the discipline. If you want to roast a medley, a fabulous feast to put in the centre of the table near Christmas so that guests can pull at legs and carve off breast meat like medieval kings, check the timings for each type of game bird then throw them, buttered, into the oven one after the other, with one eye on the clock.

Approximate cooking times for game birds with the oven at 190°C/Gas Mark 5. Make sure the oven is properly preheated.
Pheasant: 40–50 minutes
Grouse: 35–45 minutes
Mallard: 35–45 minutes
Partridge: 25–35 minutes
Woodcock: 15–20 minutes
Snipe: 15–20 minutes

streaky bacon, cut very thin

a selection of game birds (e.g. 2 pheasant, 3 partridge, 1 wild duck and assorted smaller birds such as woodcock and snipe)

salt and freshly ground black pepper

softened unsalted butter

for the gravy

1 onion, peeled and sliced

½ stick of celery, chopped

1 small carrot, chopped

1 sprig thyme

1 bay leaf

2 tablespoons butter

1 glass red wine

300 ml chicken stock

Usually a butcher will prepare the birds ready for the oven but, if not, wrap or tie a little of the streaky bacon around them, season with salt and pepper and rub with butter. Place the bird (or birds) that take the longest time to cook on a roasting tray and put in the oven. Gradually add the other game birds – timing each one. Keep in mind that you will be opening the oven door often so you may need to increase the cooking time by a few minutes. Remove from the oven when cooked, place on a warmed dish and cover with foil while you make the gravy. Snip off the last joint of the wings and add to the roasting pan with the vegetables, herbs and butter. Cook until soft, then add the wine. Scrape away at the base of the pan to lift the bits that are stuck to it, then add the stock. Bring to the boil and cook for a few minutes. Serve the game birds with gravy and bread sauce (see Fergus Henderson's recipe on page 44) along with steamed purple sprouting broccoli and warmed game chips (use hand-fried crisps like Tyrrell's or Burt's).

Wild duck stuffed with cranberries, corn bread, pumpkin seeds and onion by Rose Prince

SERVES 4–6

Waterfowl and cranberries – you could be on the wetlands of Massachusetts themselves. Ask the butcher to bone the mallard for you, but do give them plenty of warning.

2 tablespoons butter

2 medium onions, very finely chopped

2 sticks of celery, finely sliced

I Cox's apple, grated

juice of half a lemon

I pinch of dried thyme

½ teaspoon fresh ground black pepper

½ teaspoon soft sea salt

120 g dried cranberries

2 large slices of corn or sourdough bread, cut into small cubes

2 tablespoons green pumpkin seeds

I egg, beaten

2 wild duck, boned but the legs left intact

natural parcel string

Preheat the oven to 220°C/Gas Mark 7. Melt the butter in a pan and cook the onions and celery until soft. Add the apple with the lemon juice, thyme, pepper, salt and cranberries. Stir fry for a minute then add the bread and pumpkin seeds and cook for a further minute. Remove from the heat and allow to cool. Stir in the egg.

Lay the ducks out on a board, flesh side up. Spoon the cranberry stuffing on to the centre of each duck. Mallards vary in size so only spoon enough to fill the duck; too much and it will be impossible to truss. Wrap the duck around the stuffing in a parcel then tie with string in two places, tucking in the legs as you do so.

Roast the duck for 40–50 minutes. Test for doneness by sticking a skewer into the centre of the duck for 1 minute then feeling its temperature. If the skewer is hot the stuffing is cooked. Slice and serve with wild rice or roast potatoes.

Chestnut stuffing

ENOUGH FOR A 4.5 KG BIRD

This is stuffing made from a mixture of Sierra produce – chestnuts, apples and dried figs.

5 rashers of bacon, chopped

2 cloves of garlic, chopped

I large onion, chopped

I apple, chopped

100 g dried figs, chopped

25 g dried porcini mushrooms, chopped and rehydrated in warm water

zest of I lemon

400 g peeled chestnuts, chopped

200 g several-days-old breadcrumbs

I egg, beaten

salt and pepper to season

In a pan, sauté the bacon, garlic, onion, apple, figs, mushrooms and lemon for about 10 minutes. Add the chopped chestnuts, breadcrumbs and beaten egg and mix thoroughly. Add a little water if the stuffing mixture is too dry. Now stuff the bird in the usual way. Before serving make sure that the stuffing is cooked all the way through.

Rosemary quail with Camargue red rice and spiced black beluga lentils

SERVES 4

Once the shooting season finishes, the only pheasant and partridge to be had will need defrosting. A delicious alternative is a brace of quail.

175 g Camargue red rice
chicken stock (optional)
8 quail
8 sprigs of rosemary, about 15 cm long
extra-virgin olive oil
1 onion, finely diced
4 cloves of garlic, finely diced
1 red chilli, finely diced
2 star anise
1 teaspoon turmeric
seeds from 2 cardamom pods
100 g beluga lentils
vegetable stock (optional)
handful fresh coriander, finely chopped
chilli-infused extra-virgin olive oil
1 lemon
soy sauce
butter

Preheat the oven to 200°C (or 190 C for fan ovens)/Gas Mark 6. Boil the Camargue red rice in water (or chicken stock) for 30 minutes, remove from the heat and leave to stand for a further 15–20 minutes, according to the desired texture. Cut the bushy tops off the rosemary sprigs and place them inside the birds with some showing. Spread the remaining rosemary on the bottom of a roasting dish and place the quail on top. Season with salt and pepper and drizzle with extra-virgin olive oil. Roast for 20 minutes and allow to stand for two minutes before serving. Meanwhile, sweat the onion, garlic, chilli, star anise, turmeric and cardamom seeds in a little olive oil. Add the lentils and twice the volume of water or vegetable stock. Bring to the boil and simmer for 20 minutes or until soft. Remove the anise and add the coriander. Dress with a little chilli-infused olive oil and lemon juice. Add a hint of soy sauce and butter to the rice, and stir. Serve with the lentils and quail.

Sauce for all sorts of wild fowls
by Sarah Clayton, 1730

1 small onion, chopped
12 peppercorns
25 g butter
2 anchovy fillets
300 ml claret or other red wine
300 ml chicken or beef stock

Fry the onion and peppercorns in a little butter, add the anchovies and fry for a minute or two longer. Pour in the wine, bubble for a couple of minutes, add the stock and simmer for an hour or so, adding a little water if necessary. Strain and pour into a serving dish.

Chestnut, walnut, apple and celery stuffing

3 tablespoons olive oil

I onion, finely chopped

3–4 sticks of celery, chopped

110 g walnuts, chopped

I apple, peeled, cored and chopped

450 g tin unsweetened chestnut purée

450 g sausage meat

225 g brown bread crumbs

2 eggs, beaten

½ bunch flat-leaf parsley, chopped

salt and freshly ground black pepper

450 g vacuum-packed chestnuts, quartered

Heat the oil in a frying pan over a gentle heat. Add the onion, celery, walnuts and apple and fry until golden and softened, stirring to prevent sticking. Put the mixture into a large bowl and add the remaining ingredients, mixing well, ideally with your hands. Use to stuff a bird (this goes very well with roast turkey) or cook separately while the meat is roasting. Cook for at least 30 minutes or until brown and crispy on top.

Winter sauce

A close relative of the sauce made famous by Harry's Bar in Venice, where carpaccio was invented. This is the sauce created by pig-farmer Richard Vaughan to be served with pork.

200 g mayonnaise

3 tablespoons chicken stock

a few drops of Tabasco sauce

a dash of Worcestershire sauce

70 g mustard (English or French)

Whisk all the ingredients together until you have a thick double-cream consistency.

Vegetables
Braised chicory with butter and
lemon juice by Rose Prince

SERVES 4

You will need a wide, heavy-based pan with a
lid for this dish, which is good with fried fish,
roast poultry or lamb.

60 g unsalted butter
4 chicory, split lengthways
a few thyme leaves
the juice of 1 lemon

Melt the butter in a pan over a medium heat. Lay
the chicory cut side down in the pan, season with
salt and pepper and add the thyme leaves. Cook
for a few minutes, add the lemon juice and cover.
Continue cooking for about 20 minutes over a low
heat. Keep an eye on them – they should brown
underneath but not burn. Turn the chicory carefully
in the pan; serve warm.

Cheese and chicory salad
by Rose Prince

SERVES 4

Nothing could be simpler – the slightly
bitter leaves, the nuts and cheese in a salad
with a sweet and sour mustard dressing. You
can interchange the cheeses and nuts, using
walnuts or pinenuts, hard or blue cheeses.
A fresh goat's cheese makes a light summer
version.

leaves from 3 red chicory, cut into strips lengthways
180 g hard, mature cheese, pared with a potato peeler
2 tablespoons crushed hazelnuts, or fresh hazelnuts when available
for the dressing
6 tablespoons olive oil
2 tablespoons red wine vinegar
1 tablespoon Dijon mustard
1 teaspoon golden caster sugar
4 teaspoons soft crystal sea salt
2 tablespoons water
4 shallots, finely chopped
freshly ground black pepper

Combine the salad ingredients in a large bowl.
Whisk together the dressing ingredients until
emulsified, then pour over the salad. Turn a couple
of times with a spoon and serve.

Lemony lentils

SERVES 2

---

100 g puy lentils

1 small onion, finely chopped

quarter of an unwaxed lemon, finely chopped

1 bay leaf

2 cloves of garlic, chopped

1 small piece of cinnamon

1 small piece of star anise (about two petals)

400 ml water

1 teaspoon soy sauce

2 lemon wedges, to serve

Put all the ingredients, except the soy sauce and lemon wedges, into a saucepan, bring to the boil and simmer gently for about 25 minutes, until the lentils are soft but not collapsing. If the mixture looks too watery, raise the temperature slightly and boil away some of the liquid. Add the soy sauce, stir and serve with a wedge of fresh lemon.

Spicy chickpeas and shallots

SERVES 6

Ideal as a side dish; the prunes add velvetiness.

---

2 tablespoons olive oil

25 g unsalted butter

8–10 medium-size banana shallots, peeled and finely sliced into rings

1 teaspoon cumin seeds

10 pitted prunes, soaked for an hour or so and cut into quarters

1 teaspoon ground coriander

1 teaspoon cinnamon

1 tablespoon ground cumin

1 teaspoon sugar

400 g tin chickpeas

Put the oil and butter into a large frying pan and heat over a medium heat. Sauté the shallots with the cumin seeds and a pinch of salt until very soft. Add a few tablespoons of water if they get too dry. It will take about 15 minutes. Add the soft soaked prunes, coriander, cinnamon, cumin and sugar. Then add the drained chickpeas and season. Fry for a further two minutes. Serve in a warm bowl.

Aligot
by Rose Prince

SERVES AT LEAST 4

A big copper pan adds to the success of this dish – aligot must be served straight from the pan.

800 g white floury potatoes, peeled

2 tablespoons softened unsalted butter

I small clove of garlic, grated

2 tablespoons crème fraîche

600 g tomme cheese, chopped into small squares

Boil the potatoes in salted water until tender, then drain and put through a mouli-légumes or potato ricer. Put the potatoes back in the pan over a very low heat. Add the butter, garlic and crème fraîche and beat with a wooden spoon. Add the cheese a handful at a time, stirring constantly in a figure-of-eight pattern (local cooks insist on this). Once all the cheese is incorporated, taste for salt and serve immediately with slices of rare roast beef.

Steamed seakale, truffles and walnut-oil dressing by Rose Prince

SERVES 4

In spring and summer the black truffles in this recipe can be replaced with shavings of summer truffle, a white-ish, earthy-textured truffle that is less pungent – and therefore less expensive. The dish is also good with morels, a springtime wild fungi (for suppliers of truffles and morels see page 204).

450 g fresh seakale

4 tablespoons walnut oil

I tablespoon cider vinegar

I pinch sugar

½ teaspoon Dijon mustard

I teaspoon water

leaves from 4 sprigs of flat-leaf parsley, chopped

leaves from I punnet of red basil sprouts

I small black 'melanosporum' truffle

It should not be necessary to trim the seakale, just brush away any sand or grit or wash if necessary. Bring a pan of water to the boil and place the kale in a steamer basket above it. Cover and steam over the boiling water for 3–5 minutes until just tender. Remove from the pan and drain on a dry cloth. Put the oil, vinegar, sugar, mustard and water into a bowl and whisk. Pour the dressing over the kale, add the parsley and sprouts, then turn over a few times. Divide among four plates, shave slices of truffle over each one, then season with sea salt and freshly ground black pepper.

Puddings
Winter pudding, or rhubarb charlotte with freezer raspberries
by Rose Prince

SERVES 6

This is a toasted winter version of summer pudding, filled with a classic mix of rhubarb and raspberries. Freezer raspberries, grown in Britain, are a wonderful source of winter fruit. Plentiful and cheap, these are berries free of air-freight and fossil-fuel issues.

700 g rhubarb, cut in 2 cm pieces

400 g freezer raspberries

golden caster sugar

6 slices of day-old or stale white sliced bread, trimmed and cut into four triangles

softened, unsalted butter

ground cinnamon

Preheat the oven to 200°C/Gas Mark 6. Put the rhubarb and the raspberries into a pan and cook over a low heat until the rhubarb is soft. Add enough sugar to sweeten to your taste, then pour into a 5-cm-deep gratin dish. Butter the bread pieces on one side, and arrange on top of the stewed fruit. Sprinkle a pinch of cinnamon over the surface. Bake in the oven for half an hour, or until the edges of the bread are golden brown. Scatter a little sugar over the surface. Serve the pudding hot or at room temperature, with fresh custard or thick double cream.

Rice kheer

SERVES 4–6

This is a simple rice pudding eaten as a festival dish during the harvest, made by Dr Nandini Seshadri, the head of Tilda's DNA lab in Delhi. She uses 'brokens' to make it, basmati that has been damaged during milling.

90 g pure basmati rice ('brokens' are available in Asian supermarkets)

1 litre full cream milk

8–10 threads of saffron

120 g golden caster sugar

1 pinch ground cardamom

5–7 pistachios, chopped

5–7 almonds, blanched and chopped

Wash the rice. Soak in plenty of water for 20 minutes, then drain and set aside. Heat half the milk with the saffron, add the rice and stir until it reaches boiling point. Reduce the heat and simmer until it is just tender. Add the remaining milk with the sugar, cardamom, pistachios and almonds. Bring back to the boil, stirring gently but continuously. Reduce heat, simmer for 2–3 minutes and serve hot.

Plum pudding

MAKES 2 LARGE PUDDINGS

This recipe from *Elizabeth David's Christmas* originally came from the *Ocklye Cookery Book*, a pre-1914 family recipe book. David writes: 'Friends who have used the Ocklye Christmas pudding recipe have been well pleased with it. Note that no sugar is required. The pudding is all the better for the omission, the dried fruit providing more than enough of its own natural sweetness.'

I kg raisins
I kg currants
170 g candied peel, finely chopped
13 eggs
850 ml of milk (you can replace 300 ml of the milk with stout if you wish)
14 teacupsful of breadcrumbs
700 g plain flour
700 g finely chopped suet
3 wineglasses of brandy
2 wineglasses of rum

Mix these ingredients well together, put into buttered basins, and boil for 14 hours. For mixing the pudding you need a really capacious bowl and a stout wooden spoon – and as everybody in the family is supposed to take a hand in the job, this part of it should not be very hard work. It's all done on the day before the puddings are supposed to be cooked, and the mixture is left overnight in the covered bowl, in a cool place. Some people think it a mistake to add the brandy, rum and stout at this point, but it's easier to do all the mixing in one go. In a single night the fruit isn't going to start fermenting. The ritual silver coins, ring, thimble and other pudding favours can be put into each pudding when the basins are packed – they're supposed to be wrapped in greaseproof paper, more so that they can be found than for hygienic reasons. But if there are children it's better to slip them surreptitiously on the plates when the pudding is served so that they are easily seen. The drama of inadvertently swallowed coins and charms is something one can do without on Christmas Day. The pudding will swell during cooking, so allow for this by leaving 2–3 cm of space at the top when the mixture is packed into the buttered basins. Cover each pudding with buttered greaseproof paper before tying on the cloths.

On Christmas Day: Elizabeth David advises steaming the pudding for a good 2 hours on the day, then allowing it to stand for 10 minutes before turning it out on to a plate and pouring over warmed rum or brandy that has been lit with a match.

Bitter orange and sweet milk pudding

SERVES 6

180 g natural whole-milk yogurt
juice of three bitter oranges
480 g condensed milk
3 tablespoons Seville orange marmalade
red pips from one pomegranate

Whisk together the yogurt, orange juice and condensed milk, then fold in the marmalade. Pour into a bowl and refrigerate. Serve with the pomegranate pips scattered on top.

Rhubarb tart with ginger custard

SERVES 8–10

Shaun Hill, who began his culinary career working for Robert Carrier, is best known for his restaurant The Merchant House in the food-oriented town of Ludlow. The Merchant House served its last hors d'oeuvre a couple of years ago and Hill is now co-partner in the Glasshouse brasserie just up the road in Worcester. This is his recipe for Rhubarb tart and ginger custard.

for the sweet pastry
2 medium-size egg yolks
150 g butter
1 heaped tablespoon caster sugar
275 g plain flour
for the filling
1 kg forced rhubarb
150 g caster sugar
2 medium-size egg yolks
75 ml double cream
for the custard
5 medium-size egg yolks
50 g caster sugar
275 ml milk
40 g crystallised ginger, chopped

To make the pastry: beat together the egg yolks, butter and sugar, then stir in the flour. Knead once or twice to make sure everything is well mixed. Rest the pastry for an hour. Heat an oven to 200°C/Gas Mark 6, then line a 26-cm flan case with the pastry and bake blind for 15 minutes.
To make the filling: cut the rhubarb into 3 cm lengths. Cook in a saucepan with 100 g of the sugar until the rhubarb is cooked but still firm – about

4 minutes. Transfer this on to the cooked flan case. Whisk the two egg yolks with the remaining 50 g sugar and the cream and pour this over the rhubarb. Return the tart to the oven and bake for 40 minutes.
To make the custard: whisk together the yolks and sugar. Heat the milk and ginger to boiling point then whisk on to the egg and sugar mixture. Return the custard to the saucepan and cook very gently until it starts to thicken – about 10 minutes. Don't let it boil.

Rhubarb fool

SERVES 4

See suppliers on page 204 for coloured sugar crystals.

500 g rhubarb, cut into 2 cm pieces
150 g golden caster sugar
300 ml whipping cream
demerara sugar or coloured sugar crystals for dusting
Moroccan rose petals

Cook the rhubarb with the sugar and a splash of water until soft. Allow to cool, then refrigerate. Just before serving, fold in the cream and spoon into a glass bowl or individual glass dishes. Dust with a little demerara or coloured sugar crystals and some Moroccan rose petals.

Winter dried fruit salad

SERVES 6

In this recipe from Pippa Small, the rosewater will bring out the best in the fruit and envelop your guests in a swooningly rich scent.

zest of 1 lemon

200 g granulated sugar

250 g dried organic apricots

100 g organic dried dates, stoned

200 g organic dried figs, halved

200 g each of dried pears and peaches, halved

100 g dried organic cranberries

1–2 vanilla pods

a few cardamom pods

2–4 tablespoons rosewater

1 ripe pomegranate, halved and seeds removed

Place the zest, sugar and 450 ml water in a non-corrosive pan. Dissolve the sugar over a low heat, then add the dried fruits, vanilla and cardamom, and simmer gently for 10 minutes. Add the rosewater, then cover, remove from the heat and leave to infuse for half an hour or so. To serve, spoon into a dish and top the fruit salad with the seeds from the pomegranate.

Chocolate
Nick Jones' Mum's chocolate pot

SERVES 8

Nick Jones, who is married to Desert Island discs presenter and newsreader Kirsty Young, owns Soho House in London and New York. His mother devised this recipe for chocolate mousse. The Joneses serve it in tiny espresso cups – just about the right amount because it is amazingly rich.

4 pints of double cream

2 large slabs of Bourneville chocolate

dash of Grand Marnier

In a saucepan, warm the cream over a low heat. Break the chocolate into lumps and melt it in the cream. Stir until all the chocolate is melted. Add the Grand Marnier and stir. Pour the mixture into small pots or espresso cups and place in the fridge 24 hours before they are needed.

Chocolate cake

Claudia Roden's family fled to the UK from Cairo in the Fifties, bringing nothing with them. Her kitchen in her family home in Hampstead, north London, is therefore surprisingly European, terracotta tiled and white walled, shelves stacked with French porcelain, her table made by Johnny Gray, Elizabeth David's nephew – the whole effect seems to be admirably summed up by her recipe for English chocolate cake with a twist...

250 g dark bitter chocolate

170 g butter

6 eggs, separated

6 tablespoons sugar

100 g ground almonds

zest of 1 orange (optional)

Preheat the oven to 180°C/Gas Mark 4. Melt the chocolate in a small pan placed in a larger pan of boiling water. Add the butter and let it melt. Beat the egg yolks with the sugar till pale. Add the ground almonds and the melted chocolate and butter, and mix well. Beat the egg whites stiff and fold them in. Grease a 25 cm non-stick cake tin with butter and dust with flour. Pour the cake mixture in and bake in the oven for 45–60 minutes. You can add the grated zest of one orange just before you fold in the egg whites

Chestnut and chocolate truffles

by Jane Cumberbatch

MAKES ABOUT 36

100 g butter, cut into small pieces

100 g sugar

200 g chocolate with 70 per cent cocoa

200 g peeled chestnuts, chopped

3 egg yolks

200 ml double cream

cocoa powder

In a pan over a low heat, melt the butter, sugar and chocolate. Mix thoroughly. Leave to cool for 30 minutes and then add the chestnuts, egg yolks and cream. Mix thoroughly and refrigerate for a couple of hours until firmish. Remove from the fridge and, for each truffle, scoop 2 teaspoons of mixture to roll into a roughly shaped ball. Place on a foil-lined baking sheet and chill overnight. Roll in cocoa powder just before serving.

Marmalade
Dora's Seville orange marmalade

MAKES ABOUT SIX 240 G POTS

Dora Fraga, who farms in Seville, Andalucia, makes her marmalade in the British way, as soon as the fruit ripens. She insists that the earlier in the season you make marmalade, the fresher the flavour and the better it sets. Shred the peel by hand if possible; marmalade is so much better when there is plenty of contrast between jelly and peel. Wax discs and cellophane covers are available in kitchen shops.

750 g bitter Seville oranges

2.2 litres water

juice of 1 lemon

granulated or preserving sugar

6 jars, heated in the oven to sterilise

Wash the oranges, cut them in half, then squeeze the juice into a large bowl. Reserve the pips and tie them in a muslin bag. Cut the orange peel into thin shreds and add to the bowl with the water, bag of pips and lemon juice. Soak for 24–48 hours to tenderise. Put it all into a large pan and bring to the boil. Cook for 1–1¼ hours, until the peel is soft to the bite. Remove the bag of pips, squeezing gently. Take the pan off the heat and measure out the contents into a large bowl using a measuring jug. For every 600 ml of liquid, add 480 g sugar. Stir until dissolved. Pour the mixture back into the pan and bring to the boil until setting point is reached. Setting point is when a little marmalade, spooned on to a cold plate and allowed to cool, has a set surface and wrinkles when pushed with a finger. Pour into jam jars, seal with a wax disc and cover with cellophane, securing with a rubber band.

Breads
Three-minute spelt bread

With spelt there is no need to let the dough rise. This really takes three minutes to prepare.

500 g spelt flour
10 g fast-acting dried yeast
½ teaspoon sea salt
50 g sunflower seeds
50 g sesame seeds
50 g linseeds
500 ml warm water

Preheat the oven to 200°C/Gas Mark 6. Combine all the ingredients, adding the water last. Mix well and turn the dough into a greased loaf tin. Put straight into the oven and bake for 1 hour. Remove the loaf, turn it out of the tin and then return it to the oven without the tin for a further 5–10 minutes.

Lentil rolls

Dan Lepard's delicious wares can be sampled at his delicatessen Ottolenghi in London. Or you can make your own... The dry, peppery taste of lentils suits this light rye dough, as the astringency of the rye brightens the otherwise dusty flavour in the same way as a squeeze of lemon juice over a lentil salad. Here the lentils are cooked until they are very soft before being added to the dough, so they combine well and bake without stealing moisture. Slightly sweet and softly tender inside, these dinner rolls are good with broth-based soups. Freeze in an airtight container as soon as they are cold, and simply reheat for 10–12 minutes.

200 g well-cooked puy or green lentils, drained
100 ml water at about 20°C
½ sachet easy-blend yeast
1 tablespoon runny honey
200 g strong white flour
50 g rye (or spelt/wholemeal) flour
¾ level teaspoon fine sea salt
olive oil and sea-salt flakes to finish

Beat the lentils with the water, yeast and honey. In a large bowl mix the white and rye flours with the salt, then pour in the lentil yeast. Mix together until you have an evenly combined, sticky dough, adding a little more water if needed. Cover the bowl and leave for 10 minutes. Pour a teaspoon of oil on to the work surface. Knead the dough on the oiled surface for 10 seconds, ending with the dough in a smooth round ball. Give the bowl a quick clean with warm water, then dry and rub lightly with another teaspoon of oil. Place the dough back in the bowl and leave for a further 10 minutes. Remove the dough, knead once more, returning the shape of the dough to a smooth, round ball. Place it back in the bowl, cover and leave for an hour in a warm place. Lightly flour the work surface and roll the dough into a sheet measuring 25 cm x 20 cm. Lay this on a tray lined with a flour-dusted cloth, then cover the surface of the dough with another cloth and leave for 1 hour, or until almost doubled in height. Preheat the oven to 220°C/Gas Mark 7. Uncover the dough and cut it into 16 squares, four across by four down. Brush the tops lightly with olive oil, then place them on a flour-dusted baking tray. Sprinke a few salt flakes over and bake on the centre shelf of the oven for 25 minutes, or until the rolls are pale brown and feel light. Cover the rolls with a cloth as soon as they are out of the oven to keep them soft and moist.

Moroccan ksra

MAKES A 1 KG LOAF

Pippa Small's tasty flatbread is usually made to be eaten with tagine, a spicy Moroccan stew.

300 g strong white bread flour

300 g fine semolina flour

¼ tablespoon anise seeds

¼ teaspoon fine sea salt

1 teaspoon active dried yeast

380 ml warm water

2 tablespoons olive oil, plus 1 tablespoon to brush when baking

1 tablespoon sesame seeds (optional)

Place the flours, anise seeds and salt in a large mixing bowl. Dissolve the yeast in the water and then pour the oil into the water. Pour the yeast mixture into the flour and mix with your fingers, or a wooden spoon, to form a dough. Transfer to a floured surface and knead well. Continue kneading for about 5 minutes until the dough is soft and elastic. Shape into a large ball, then flatten to a 2 cm thickness. Place it on a lightly floured baking sheet. Cover with a towel, and let it rise for 2–3 hours until double in size. Preheat the oven to 200°C/Gas Mark 6. Brush the top of the loaf with olive oil and sprinkle with sesame seeds if you like. Prick the top of the loaf all over using a fork. Bake for 20–25 minutes, or until the loaf is golden and sounds hollow when tapped. Serve warm or cool.

White soda bread

Darina Allen says: 'Soda bread only takes 2 or 3 minutes to make and 20–30 minutes to bake. It is certainly another of my "great convertibles". We have had the greatest fun experimenting with different variations and uses. It's also great with olives, sun-dried tomatoes or caramelized onions added, so the possibilities are endless for the hitherto humble soda bread."

450 g white flour, preferably unbleached

1 level teaspoon salt

1 level teaspoon breadsoda

sour milk or buttermilk to mix (approximately 350–412 ml)

First, fully preheat your oven to 230°C/Gas Mark 8. Sieve the dry ingredients into a bowl and make a well in the centre. Pour most of the milk in at once. Using one hand, mix in the flour from the sides of the bowl, adding more milk if necessary. The dough should be softish, not too wet and sticky. When it all comes together, turn it out on to a well floured work surface. Wash and dry your hands. Tidy the dough up and flip it over gently. Pat it into a round about 2.5 cm deep and cut a cross on it to let the fairies out! Let the cuts go over the sides of the bread to make sure of this. Bake for 15 minutes, then turn the oven down to Gas Mark 6/200°C for 30 minutes or until the bread is cooked. If you are in doubt, tap the bottom of the bread: if it is cooked it will sound hollow.

Conversion table

Weight (solids)

7g	¼oz
10g	½oz
20g	¾oz
25g	1oz
40g	1½oz
50g	2oz
60g	2½oz
75g	3oz
100g	3½oz
110g	4oz (¼lb)
125g	4½oz
150g	5½oz
175g	6oz
200g	7oz
225g	8oz (½lb)
250g	9oz
275g	10oz
300g	10½oz
310g	11oz
325g	11½oz
350g	12oz (¾lb)
375g	13oz
400g	14oz
425g	15oz
450g	1lb
500g (½kg)	18oz
600g	1¼lb
700g	1½lb
750g	1lb 10oz
900g	2lb

1kg	2¼lb
1.1kg	2½lb
1.2kg	2lb 12oz
1.3kg	3lb
1.5kg	3lb 5oz
1.6kg	3½lb
1.8kg	4lb
2kg	4lb 8oz
2.25kg	5lb
2.5kg	5lb 8oz
3kg	6lb 8oz

Volume (liquids)

5ml	1 teaspoon
10ml	1 dessertspoon
15ml	1 tablespoon or ½fl oz
30ml	1fl oz
40ml	1½fl oz
50ml	2fl oz
60ml	2½fl oz
75ml	3fl oz
100ml	3½fl oz
125ml	4fl oz
150ml	5fl oz (¼ pint)
160ml	5½fl oz
175ml	6fl oz
200ml	7fl oz
225ml	8fl oz
250ml (0.25 litre)	9fl oz
300ml	10fl oz (½ pint)
325ml	11fl oz
350ml	12fl oz
370ml	13fl oz

400ml	14fl oz
425ml	15fl oz (¾ pint)
450ml	16fl oz
500ml (0.5 litre)	18fl oz
550ml	19fl oz
600ml	20fl oz (1 pint)
700ml	1¼ pints
850ml	1½ pints
1 litre	1¾ pints
1.2 litres	2 pints
1.5 litres	2½ pints
1.8 litres	3 pints
2 litres	3½ pints

Length

5mm	¼ in
1cm	½ in
2cm	¾ in
2.5cm	1in
3cm	1¼ in
4cm	1½ in
5cm	2in
7.5cm	3in
10cm	4in
15cm	6in
18cm	7in
20cm	8in
24cm	10in
28cm	11in
30cm	12in

Suppliers

Carrot butter, a sauce for fish
Purslane is available from **Secretts**
tel: 01483 520500
website: www.secretts.co.uk

Celery, crayfish and potato salad
Freshwater crayfish from Wiltshire streams are
available from **Everleigh Farm Shop Ltd**
tel: 01264 850344
website: www.everleighfarmshop.co.uk

**Fresh goat's cheese and beetroot salad with red
wine vinegar and walnut vinaigrette**
Monte Enebro is available from **Brindisa**
tel: 020 7407 1036
website: www.brindisa.com

Lavender Trust cupcakes
Lavender sugar is available from **Hanbury Foods**
tel: 01179 773474
website: www.hanburyfoods.com
Grape violet food-colouring paste is available from
Jane Asher
tel: 020 7584 6177
website: www.janeasher.com

Remoulade with air-dried mutton
Herdwick mutton is available from various farmers,
including **Andrew Sharp**
tel: 01229 588299
website: www.farmersharp.co.uk

Sitka seafood stew
Cornish spider crabmeat or white meat from
brown crabs is available from **Matthew Stevens &
Son**

tel: 01736 799392
website: www.mstevensandson.co.uk

**Spicy barbecued langoustines with lemon
and garlic**
Premium Japanese sake is available from **Isake**,
Fortnum & Mason, Harvey Nichols, Harrods and
Selfridges.
website: www.isake.co.uk

**Steamed seakale, truffles and walnut-oil
dressing**
Truffles and morels are both available from **Wild
Harvest**
tel: 0202 7498 5397
website: www.wildharvestuk.com

Tomato and red chard salad
Young red chard leaves are available from **Secretts**
tel: 01483 520500
website: www.secretts.co.uk

Venison Napoleon
Macsween haggis is available throughout the UK.
Contact **Macsween of Edinburgh**
tel: 0131 440 2555
website: www.macsween.co.uk

Venison with plum wine and salted plum paste
Japanese plum wine is available from **Mount Fuji**
tel: 01743 741169
website: www.mountfuji.co.uk

almonds, Fig and almond tart 108
anchovies
    Anchoïade 40
    Parsley, anchovy and black olive sauce 103
    Saddle of fallow deer with anchovies 135
apples
    Apple and blackberry pie 158
    Apple and blueberry crumble 157
    Apple snow 53
    Apple and walnut cake 162
    Baked Johanna Gold apples 155
    Chestnut, walnut, apple and celery stuffing 187
    Pain perdu aux pommes 154
    Windfall toffee apples 157
artichokes
    Confit of artichokes 95
    Lamb with peas, broad beans, artichoke
       hearts and roast garlic 92
asparagus
    Broad bean salad 69
    Lamb with peas, broad beans, artichoke
       hearts and roast garlic 92
    Orzotto con le primizie, barley 'risotto' with
       spring vegetables 33
    Pecorino shortbreads with new season
       asparagus 16
    Poached asparagus with shallot and mustard
       vinaigrette 14
    Scrambled eggs with goat's cheese and green
       asparagus 17
aubergines
    Tomato and ewe's-milk cheese timbales 58
    Tumbet 99
avocados, Roasted lobster salad 85

bacon, liver and 181
barley, Orzotto con le primizie, barley 'risotto'
  with spring vegetables 33
beans
    Broad bean salad 69
    Cassoulet of haricot beans 134
    Habas fritas con jamón 100
    Lamb with peas, broad beans, artichoke
       hearts and roast garlic 92
    Potée champenoise 142
    Sam and Sam's chicken salad 72
    Szechuan green beans 57
beef
    Beef tartare and horseradish 93
    Steak 134
beetroot
    Fresh goat's cheese and beetroot salad 13
    Rocket, mint, beetroot and feta salad 10
blackberries, Apple and blackberry pie 158
blueberries
    Apple and blueberry crumble 157
    Blueberries with lime sugar 50
bread
    Bread sauce 44
    Brioche 56
    Crab crostini 58
    Lentil rolls 200
    Moroccan ksra 202
    Pain perdu aux pommes 154
    Pappa al pomodoro 65
    Peperonata bruschetta 61
    Sweet potato bread 162
    Three-minute spelt bread 200
    White soda bread 202

cabbage
    Colcannon 146
    Partridge with cabbage 142
    Potée champenoise 142
cakes
    Apple and walnut cake 162
    Chocolate brownies 161
    Chocolate cake 198
    Lavender Trust cupcakes 115
    St John caraway seed cake 113
    Traditional scones 113
carrots
    Carrot butter 32
    Grated carrot and poppy seed salad 75
cauliflower, Lancashire cauliflower cheese 151
celeriac, Remoulade with air-dried mutton 171
celery
    Celery, crayfish and potato salad 10
    Celery heart and wild mushroom savoury
       baked custard 123
    Chestnut, walnut, apple and celery stuffing 187
    Duck and celery soup 121
chard, Swiss chard and potatoes 147
cheese
    Aligot 190
    Baked peaches with ricotta 107
    Caesar salad 69
    Cheddar and tarragon soufflé 129
    Cheese and chicory salad 188
    Cheese straws 161
    Fresh goat's cheese and beetroot salad 13
    Herb tart 61
    Lancashire cauliflower cheese 151
    Pear, Parmesan and truffle salad 124
    Pecorino shortbreads with new season
       asparagus 16
    Potato torta with ricotta, Parmesan and basil
       37
    Prosciutto, watercress and Manchego cheese
       on grilled sourdough bread 13
    Raspberries with ricotta 104
    Ravioloni con radicchio e ricotta 79
    Red peppers stuffed with Gorgonzola 98
    Rocket, mint, beetroot and feta salad 10
    Scrambled eggs with goat's cheese and green
       asparagus 17
    Summer fruits with goat's curd and East End
       honey 106
    Tomato and ewe's-milk cheese timbales 58
    Tomato and ricotta tarts 60
    Watercress and goat's cheese soup 22
Cherry clafoutis 112
chestnuts
    Chestnut and chocolate truffles 198
    Chestnut stuffing 184
    Chestnut, walnut, apple and celery stuffing 187
    Tomato, chestnut and chorizo soup 120
chicken
    Chicken breast with morels, spinach and dry
       sherry 96–7
    Georgian coronation chicken 97
    Pot-roast chicken 174
    Potée champenoise 142
    La poule au pot 180
    Sam and Sam's chicken salad 72
    Thomas Keller's simple roast chicken 44
    To dress chickens the Barbary way 43
chickpeas, Spicy chickpeas and shallots 189
chicory
    Braised chicory 188
    Cheese and chicory salad 188
    Creamed chicory soup 167
chillies
    Chilli, pistachio and rose petal sauce 102

    Fresh harissa 35
    Grilled squid with chillies 81
    Mackerel with rhubarb and chilli 168
chocolate
    Chestnut and chocolate truffles 198
    Chocolate brownies 161
    Chocolate cake 198
    Nick Jones' Mum's chocolate pot 197
cinnamon, Clotted cream and cinnamon
  ice-cream 48
courgettes
    Griddled courgette, pine nut and raisin salad
       70
    Tortilla 64
cranberries
    Cranberry and zinfandel jelly 48
    Wild duck stuffed with cranberries 184
cream-based desserts
    Clotted cream and cinnamon ice-cream 48
    Crème brûlée 53
    Gooseberry fool 104
    Hinds Head quaking puddings 46
    Honeycomb cream with hazelnut meringue 49
    Nick Jones' Mum's chocolate pot 197
    Rhubarb fool 196
    Spiced syllabub 155
curries
    Jaggery and garam masala grilled quail with
       quail biryani 178–9
    Koftas 177

dates
    Baked stuffed peaches 112
    Tagine of quail with dates 180
duck
    Duck and celery soup 121
    Duck confit 45
    Pan-roasted duck legs and potatoes 145
    Wild duck stuffed with cranberries 184

eggs
    Apple snow 53
    Crème brûlée 53
    An English lettuce salad 73
    Hinds Head quaking puddings 46
    Honeycomb cream with hazelnut meringue 49
    Masala scrambled eggs 17
    Pan-fried gull's eggs with sea trout and
       horseradish 19
    Scrambled eggs with goat's cheese and green
       asparagus 17
    Sweet potato latkes with poached egg,
       smoked salmon and smoked paprika
       crème fraîche 125
    Tortilla 64
    Elderflower fritters 110
falafel, golden linseed 100
fennel
    Braised fennel 36
    Pasta with sardines 80
    Pork belly with fennel, garlic and Marsala 171
    Spider crab with bronze fennel 26
figs
    Fig and almond tart 108
    Grilled figs with Bayonne ham and rocket 70
    Pigeon salad 128
fish
    Baked fish with vine-ripened tomatoes 86
    Bouillabaisse 67
    Fortune's kipper paté 170

Grilled sea bream with lemon and bay leaves 86
Grilled squid with chillies 81
Haddock poached in butter, with champ 28
Hake flavoured with garlic 131
Hot-smoked salmon with potato and leeks 170
Mackerel with rhubarb and chilli 168
Pan-fried gull's eggs with sea trout and horseradish 19
Pasta with sardines 80
Sea bass with coriander yogurt sauce and lemon purée 89
Sitka seafood stew 168
Smoked eel risotto 133
Smoked haddock and prawn pie 130
Sweet potato latkes with poached egg, smoked salmon and smoked paprika crème fraîche 125
Tomato and salmon koulibiak 81
see also shellfish
flowers, Herb, leaf and flower salad 75
fruit
Summer fruits with goat's curd and East End honey 106
Summer pudding 107
Winter dried fruit salad 197
Winter pudding, or rhubarb charlotte 193
see also fruits by name

game
Carpaccio of grouse 126
Confit of artichokes, fondant potato and wilted Good King Henry with roast venison and a lavender jus 95–6
Grouse with honey toast 141
Jaggery and garam masala grilled quail 178–9
Partridge with cabbage 142
Pheasant in the Georgian style 145
Pigeon salad 128
Roast game birds 183
Rosemary quail 186
Saddle of fallow deer 135
Sauce for all sorts of wild fowl 186
Tagine of quail with dates 180
Venison Napoleon 173
Venison with plum wine 174
Ginger custard 196
Good King Henry, Confit of artichokes, fondant potato and wilted 95
Gooseberry fool 104
grapefruit, Ceviche of minted scallops with pink 84
grapes, Tarte aux raisins 158

ham
Grilled figs with Bayonne ham and rocket 70
Habas fritas con jamón 100
Peperonata bruschetta with cured ham 61
Prosciutto, watercress and Manchego cheese on grilled sourdough bread 13
Simmered gammon 166
Harissa, Fresh 35
hazelnuts, Honeycomb cream with hazelnut meringue 49
herbs
herb butter 131
Herb, leaf and flower salad 75
Herb tart 61
Summer sauce 102
Vegetable and herb soup 20
Hinds Head quaking puddings 46

honey
Fig and almond tart with honey sauce 108
Grouse with honey toast 141
Honeycomb cream with hazelnut meringue 49
Summer fruits with goat's curd and East End honey 106
horseradish
Beef tartare and horseradish 93
Hot radish dressing 36
Pan-fried gull's eggs with sea trout and horseradish 19

ice-cream
Clotted cream and cinnamon ice-cream 48
Knickerbocker glory 50
Raspberry ice-cream 104

jelly, Cranberry and zinfandel 48
Jerusalem artichoke and herb soup 121

lamb
Confit of lamb 134
Devilled lamb's kidneys 135
Koftas 177
Lamb pavé with peas, shallot and mint 40
Lamb with peas, broad beans, artichoke hearts and roast garlic 92
Lancashire hotpot 141
Mutton slow-roasted 139–40
Overnight-baked mutton 140
Remoulade with air-dried mutton 171
Roast leg of milk-fed lamb 38
lavender
Baked peaches with ricotta 107
Lavender jus 96
Lavender Trust cupcakes 115
leeks
Hot-smoked salmon with potato and leeks 170
Leek and potato soup with poached oysters and toast 120
Leeks vinaigrette 16
lemons
Old-fashioned lemonade 115
Sea bass with coriander yogurt sauce and lemon purée 89
Spinach, lemon and turmeric soup 22
lentils
Lemony lentils 189
Lentil rolls 200
Spiced black beluga 186
limes, Blueberries with lime sugar 50
Liver and bacon 181

Mango lassi 56
marmalade, Dora's Seville orange 199
muesli, Bircher 56
mushrooms
Caramelised cep and thyme tartlets 124
Celery heart and wild mushroom savoury baked custard 123
Chicken breast with morels, spinach and dry sherry 96–7
Fresh porcini with olive oil and lemon 123
Mushroom and potato soup 118
Orzotto con le primizie, barley 'risotto' with spring vegetables 33
Risotto aux cèpes 147
Spaghettini with Scottish chanterelles 126
Tagliatelli con funghi e pancetta 128
To dress chickens the Barbary way 43
Tom yam kung 23

nougatine 106

olives, Parsley, anchovy and black olive sauce 103
onions
Onion marmalade 90
Onion soop 20
oranges
Bitter orange and sweet milk pudding 194
Dora's Seville orange marmalade 199

Pancakes 49
Parsley, anchovy and black olive sauce 103
pasta
Alice Waters' tomato confit for pasta 80
Fast spaghetti with clams 25
A fast, warming bowl of soup 166
Pasta with sardines 80
Ravioloni con radicchio e ricotta 79
Sepia pasta with prawns and chilli 79
Spaghettini with Scottish chanterelles 126
Tagliatelli con funghi e pancetta 128
peaches
Baked peaches with ricotta 107
Baked stuffed peaches 112
Pear, Parmesan and truffle salad 124
peas
Lamb pavé with peas, shallot and mint 40
Lamb with peas, broad beans, artichoke hearts and roast garlic 92
Orzotto con le primizie, barley 'risotto' with spring vegetables 33
Pea mousse 60
Pea purée 99
Potage de petits pois 68
peppers
A fast, warming bowl of soup 166
Fresh harissa 35
Peperonata bruschetta 61
Red peppers stuffed with Gorgonzola 98
Roasted lobster salad 85
Salmorejo 65
Tomato and ewe's-milk cheese timbales 58
Tumbet 99
pine nuts
Griddled courgette, pine nut and raisin salad 70
Raspberry and pine kernel tart 111
pineapple, Knickerbocker glory 50
pistachios, Chilli, pistachio and rose petal sauce 102
Plum pudding 194
polenta, Ragù di scampi with polenta integrale 29
pomegranates
Georgian coronation chicken 97
Pheasant in the Georgian style 145
pork
Crackling pork 136
Pork belly with fennel, garlic and Marsala 171
Potée champenoise 142
potatoes
Aligot 190
Baked potatoes with Gruyère and onion 151
Celery, crayfish and potato salad 10
Champ 28
Colcannon 146
Confit of artichokes, fondant potato and wilted Good King Henry 95
Hot-smoked salmon with potato and leeks 170
Leek and potato soup with poached oysters and toast 120
Mushroom and potato soup 118
Pan-roasted duck legs and potatoes 145

Potato and shellfish soup 28
Potato torta with ricotta, Parmesan and basil
   37
Roast potatoes 148
Scallion champ 146
Sliced potatoes in tian 152
Swiss chard and potatoes 147
Tumbet 99
Watercress and potato cakes with hot radish
   dressing 36
prunes, Spicy chickpeas and shallots 189
pumpkin, Spiced pumpkin soup 118

radicchio, Ravioloni con radicchio e ricotta 79
radishes
   An English lettuce salad 73
   Hot radish dressing 36
raisins, Griddled courgette, pine nut and raisin
   salad 70
raspberries
   Knickerbocker glory 50
   Raspberries with ricotta 104
   Raspberry ice-cream 104
   Raspberry and pine kernel tart 111
   Winter pudding, or rhubarb charlotte 193
rhubarb
   Mackerel with rhubarb and chilli 168
   Rhubarb fool 196
   Rhubarb tart with ginger custard 196
   Winter pudding, or rhubarb charlotte 193
rice
   Basmati pilaf with dill and cardamom 129
   Jaggery and garam masala grilled quail with
      quail biryani 178–9
   Rice kheer 193
   Risotto aux cèpes 147
   Smoked eel risotto 133
rocket
   Grilled figs with Bayonne ham and rocket 70
   Rocket, mint, beetroot and feta salad 10
rose petals, Chilli, pistachio and rose petal sauce
   102

salads
   Adeline Yen Mah's recipe for Auntie Ada's
      tofu salad 72
   Broad bean salad 69
   Caesar salad 69
   Celery, crayfish and potato salad 10
   Cheese and chicory salad 188
   An English lettuce salad 73
   Fresh goat's cheese and beetroot salad 13
   Grated carrot and poppy seed salad 75
   Griddled courgette, pine nut and raisin salad
      70
   Grilled figs with Bayonne ham and rocket 70
   Herb, leaf and flower salad 75
   Pear, Parmesan and truffle salad 124
   Pigeon salad 128
   Remoulade with air-dried mutton 171
   Roasted lobster salad 85
   Rocket, mint, beetroot and feta salad 10
   Salad of Napa Valley heirloom tomatoes 76
   Sam and Sam's chicken salad 72
   Spider crab with bronze fennel 26
sauces
   Anchoïade 40
   Bread sauce 44
   Carrot butter 32
   Chilli, pistachio and rose petal sauce 102
   Parsley, anchovy and black olive sauce 103
   Rouille 67

Sauce for all sorts of wild fowl 186
Summer sauce 102
Tomato sauce 103
Winter sauce 187
sausages
   Potée champenoise 142
   Sausage tart with onion marmalade 90
   Tomato, chestnut and chorizo soup 120
scones, traditional 113
seakale, Steamed seakale, truffles and walnut-oil
   dressing 190
shallots
   Lamb pavé with peas, shallot and mint 40
   Spicy chickpeas and shallots 189
shellfish
   Celery, crayfish and potato salad 10
   Ceviche of minted scallops with pink
      grapefruit 84
   Cocklety soup 167
   Crab crostini 58
   Cromesquis d'huîtres (fried oysters) 130
   Fast spaghetti with clams 25
   Haddock poached in butter, with champ 28
   Leek and potato soup with poached oysters
      and toast 120
   Oysters with spinach and saffron sauce 133
   Pan-fried prawns 84
   Potato and shellfish soup 28
   Potted North Atlantic prawns 25
   Ragù di scampi 29
   Roasted lobster salad 85
   Sepia pasta with prawns and chilli 79
   Shell-on prawns with scrumpy butter 89
   Sitka seafood stew 168
   Smoked haddock and prawn pie 130
   Spicy barbecued langoustines 82
   Spider crab with bronze fennel 26
   Szechuan green beans 57
   Tom yam kung 23
   Watercress soup with shellfish 23
sorrel
   Beef tartare and horseradish 93
   Sheep's-milk yogurt mousse with sorrel ice
      and nougatine 106
soufflé, Cheddar and tarragon 129
soups
   Bouillabaisse 67
   Cocklety soup 167
   Creamed chicory soup 167
   Duck and celery soup 121
   A fast, warming bowl of soup 166
   Jerusalem artichoke and herb soup 121
   Leek and potato soup with poached oysters
      and toast 120
   Mushroom and potato soup 118
   Onion soop 20
   Pappa al pomodoro 65
   Potage de petits pois 68
   Potato and shellfish soup 28
   Salmorejo 65
   Simmered gammon with watercress
      dumplings in broth 166
   Spiced pumpkin soup 118
   Spinach, lemon and turmeric soup 22
   Tom yam kung 23
   Tomato, chestnut and chorizo soup 120
   Vegetable and herb soup 20
   Watercress and goat's cheese soup 22
   Watercress soup with shellfish 23
spinach
   Chicken breast with morels, spinach and dry
      sherry 96–7

Oysters with spinach and saffron sauce 133
Spinach, lemon and turmeric soup 22
see also Good King Henry
squash
   Baked butternut, delicata or sweet dumpling
      squash 152
   Butternut squash purée 134
Summer pudding 107
sweet potatoes
   Sweet potato bread 162
   Sweet potato latkes 125
syllabub, spiced 155

tofu, Auntie Ada's tofu salad 72
tomatoes
   Alice Waters' tomato confit for pasta 80
   Baked fish with vine-ripened tomatoes 86
   Caramelised tomatoes 131
   Pan-roast tomatoes 148
   Pappa al pomodoro 65
   Peperonata bruschetta 61
   Salad of Napa Valley heirloom tomatoes 76
   Salmorejo 65
   Sam and Sam's chicken salad 72
   Tomato, chestnut and chorizo soup 120
   Tomato and ewe's-milk cheese timbales 58
   Tomato marmalade 76
   Tomato and ricotta tarts 60
   Tomato and salmon koulibiak 81
   Tomato sauce 103
   Tortilla 64
truffles
   Pear, Parmesan and truffle salad 124
   Steamed seakale, truffles and walnut-oil
      dressing 190
Tumbet 99

veal, Roast loin of veal with anchoïade 40
vegetables
   Orzotto con le primizie, barley 'risotto' with
      spring vegetables 33
   Vegetable and herb soup 20
   see also vegetables by name

walnuts
   Apple and walnut cake 162
   Auntie Ada's tofu salad 72
   Chestnut, walnut, apple and celery stuffing 187
   Fresh goat's cheese and beetroot salad 13
   Georgian coronation chicken 97
   Pheasant in the Georgian style 145
watercress
   Prosciutto, watercress and Manchego cheese
      on grilled sourdough bread 13
   Watercress dumplings 166
   Watercress and goat's cheese soup 22
   Watercress and potato cakes with hot radish
      dressing 36
   Watercress soup with shellfish 23
Winter pudding, or rhubarb charlotte 193

yogurt
   Bitter orange and sweet milk pudding 194
   Gooseberry fool 104
   Mango lassi 56
   Sea bass with coriander yogurt sauce and
      lemon purée 89
   Sheep's-milk yogurt mousse with sorrel ice and
      nougatine 106

Chefs' credits

Raymond Blanc, Le Manoir aux Quat'Saisons, Oxford (www.manoir.com): © p14 Poached asparagus; p96 Chicken breast with morels, spinach and dry sherry; p112 Cherry clafoutis; p180 La poule au pot. **Terence and Vicki Conran**, *Classic Conran* (Octopus): © p16 Leeks vinaigrette. **Rose Prince**, *The New English Kitchen* (Fourth Estate): © p10 Celery, crayfish and potato salad; p13 Fresh goat's cheese and beetroot salad; p16 Pecorino shortbreads; p17 Scrambled eggs; p23 Watercress soup with shellfish; p25 Potted North Atlantic prawns; p26 Spider crab with bronze fennel; p36 Braised fennel; p36 Watercress and potato cakes; p37 Potato torta; p40 Lamb pavé; p48 Cranberry and zinfandel jelly; p49 Honeycomb cream; p53 Apple snow; p58 Tomato and ewe's-milk cheese timbales; p60 Tomato and ricotta tarts; p61 Herb tart; p65 Salmorejo; p69 Caesar salad; p81 Tomato and salmon koulibiak; p89 Shell-on prawns; p100 Habas fritas con jamón; p104 Raspberries; p108 Fig and almond tart; p111 Elderflower fritters; p120 Leek and potato soup; p121 Duck and celery soup; p123 Celery heart and wild mushroom savoury baked custard; p129 Basmati pilaf; p130 Smoked haddock and prawn pie; p134 Confit of lamb; p139 Mutton slow-roasted; p140 Overnight-baked mutton; p141 Grouse with honey toast; p145 Pan-roasted duck legs and potatoes; p147 Swiss chard and potatoes; p151 Baked potatoes; p162 Sweet potato bread; p167 Creamed chicory soup; p168 Mackerel; p168 Sitka seafood stew; p170 Hot-smoked salmon; p183 Roast game birds; p184 Wild duck stuffed with cranberries; p188 Braised chicory; p188 Cheese and chicory salad; p190 Aligot; p190 Steamed seakale, truffles and walnut-oil dressing; p193 Winter pudding, or rhubarb charlotte; p193 Rice kheer; p194 Bitter orange and sweet milk pudding; 199 Dora's Seville orange marmalade; p200 Three-minute spelt bread. **Charlie Trotter**, Charlie Trotter's, Chicago (www.charlietrotters.com): © p13 Prosciutto, watercress and Manchego cheese. **Vineet Bhatia**, Rasoi, London (www.rasoirestaurant.co.uk): © p17 Masala scrambled eggs. **Michel Roux Jr**, Le Gavroche, London (www.le-gavroche.com): © p19 Pan-fried gull's eggs. **Michael Caines**, Gidleigh Park and Michael Caines at ABode Hotels: © p20 Vegetable and herb soup. **Heston Blumenthal**, The Fat Duck, Bray (www.fatduck.co.uk): © p20 Onion soup; p43 To dress chickens the Barbary way; p46 Hinds Head quaking pudding. **Jake Tilson**, *A Tale of 12 Kitchens* (Orion): © p22 Spinach, lemon and turmeric soup; p35 Fresh harissa. **Kirsty Young and Nick Jones**: © p22 Watercress and goat's cheese soup; p58 Crab crostini; p197 Nick Jones' Mum's chocolate pot. **Joseph Budde**, Grand Hyatt, Tokyo: © p23 Tom yam kung. **Ferran Adrià**, El Bulli, Roses (www.elbulli.com): © p25 Fast spaghetti with clams. **Richard Corrigan**, The Lindsay House, London (www.lindsayhouse.co.uk): © p28 Haddock poached in butter with champ; p32 Carrot butter. **Count Brandino and Marie Brandolini**, Naranzaria, Venice (www.naranzaria.it): © p29 Ragù di scampi; p33 Orzotto con le primizie, barley 'risotto'. **Sam and Eddy Hart**, Fino Restaurant, London (www.finorestaurant.com): © p38 Roast leg of milk fed-lamb; p99 Tumbet. **Jeremy Lee**, Blueprint Café, London (www.danddlondon.com): © p40 Roast loin of veal. **Thomas Keller**, The French Laundry, Yountville, California: © p44 Thomas Keller's simple roast chicken; p76 Salad of Napa Valley heirloom tomatoes. **Fergus Henderson**, *Nose to Tail Eating* (Bloomsbury), St John, London (www.stjohnrestaurant.com): © p44 Bread sauce; p113 St John carraway seed cake. **Simon Hopkinson**, *Roast Chicken and Other Stories* and *Second Helpings of Roast Chicken* (Ebury Press): © p45 Duck confit; p73 An English lettuce salad; p154 Pain perdu aux pommes. **Paul Gaylor**, The Lanesborough, London (www.stRegis.com): © p48 Clotted cream and cinnamon ice-cream; p113 Traditional scones. **Amy Willcock**, *The Aga Bible* (Ebury Press): © p49 Pancakes; p56 Brioche; p85 Roasted lobster salad; p90 Sausage tart; p115 Old-fashioned lemonade. **Anthony Bourdain**, *Kitchen Confidential* (Bloomsbury): © p50 Blueberries. **David Fransonet**, Moet Hennessy Chef: © p53 Crème Brûlée. **Lahore**, London: © p56 Mango lassi. **Sophie Grigson**, *Vegetables* (Harper Collins): © p57 Szechuan green beans; p61 Peperonata bruschetta; p70 Griddled courgette, pine nut and raisin salad. **Tom Aikens**, Tom Aikens, London. (www.tomaikens.co.uk): © p60 Pea Mousse; p89 Sea bass; p92 Lamb. **Sam and Sam Clark**, Moro, London (www.moro.co.uk), *Moro East* (Ebury Press): © p64 Tortilla; p72 Sam and Sam's chicken salad; p128 Pigeon salad. **Adeline Yen Mah**, *Falling Leaves* (Penguin): © p72 Adeline Yen Mah's recipe for Auntie Ada's tofu salad. © **Jamie Oliver**, 2007. All rights reserved. Fifteen, London (www.fifteen.net) p65 Pappa al pomodoro. **Franck Leibeiz**, The Cheyne Walk Brasserie, London (www.cheynewalkbrasserie.com): © p67 Bouillabaisse; p84 Pan-fried prawns with Pernod; p86 Grilled sea bream. **John Burton Race**, New Angel Restaurant, Dartmouth, Devon: © p68 Potage de petits pois; p99 Pea purée; p111 Raspberry and pine kernel tart. **Jane Packer**, Florist: © p69 Broad bean salad; p86 Baked fish with vine-ripened tomatoes. **Annie Bell**, *In My Kitchen* (Conran Octopus): © p70 Grilled figs; p79 Sepia pasta with prawns and chilli; p98 Red peppers. **Carla Tomasi** (www.gourmetontour.com): © p79 Ravioloni con radicchio e ricotta. **Alice Waters**, Chez Panisse, Berkeley, California (www.chezpanisse.com): © p80 Alice Waters' tomato confit for pasta. **Luisa Beccaria**: © p80 Pasta with sardines. **Ruth Rogers and Rose Gray**, *The River Cafe Cookbook* (Ebury Press): © p81 Grilled squid with chillies. **Paul Hughes**, Howbarrow Farm, Cumbria (www.howbarroworganic.co.uk): © p75 Herb, leaf and flower salad. **Sarah Raven**, The Cutting Garden, East Sussex, *Sarah Raven's Garden Cookbook* (Bloomsbury): © p10 Rocket, mint, beetroot and feta salad; p75 Grated carrot and poppy seed salad; p104 Raspberry ice-cream; p152 Baked butternut, delicata or sweet dumpling squash. **Mark Edwards**, Nobu, London (www.noburestaurants.com): © p82 Spicy barbecued langoustines; p174 Venison with plum wine. **Carolyn Robb**: © p84 Ceviche of minted scallops; p124 Caramelised cep and thyme tartlets. **René Redzepi**, Noma, Copenhagen (www.noma.dk): © p93 Beef tartare and horseradish; p106 Sheep's-milk yogurt mousse. **Susan Cunliffe Lister and Andrew Burton**, Swinton Park, Ripon, North Yorks (www.swintonpark.com): © p95 Confit of artichokes, fondant potato and wilted Good King Henry. **Allegra McEvedy and Henry Dimbleby**, Leon, *Leon's Ingredients and Recipes* (Conran Octopus): © p100 Golden linseed falafel; p104 Gooseberry fool. **Richard Vaughan**, Huntsham Farm, (www.huntsham.com): © p102 Summer sauce; p103 Parsley, anchovy and black olive sauce; p136 Crackling pork; p187 Winter sauce. **Pippa Small**, Jewellery maker: © p102 Chilli, pistachio and rose petal sauce; p103 Tomato sauce; p189 Spicy chickpeas and shallots; p197 Winter dried fruit salad; p202 Moroccan ksra. **Mark Hix**, Caprice Holdings (www.caprice-holdings.co.uk): © p106 Summer fruits. **Hugo Stewart and Paul Old**, Les Clos Perdus (www.lesclosperdus.com): © p107 Baked peaches with ricotta; p147 Risotto aux cèpes. **Nigella Lawson**, *How to be a Domestic Goddess* (Random House): © p115 Lavender Trust cupcakes. **Mary Contini**, Valvona Crolla, Edinburgh (www.valvonacrolla.com): © p118 Mushroom and potato soup; p128 Tagliatelli con funghi e pancetta; p126 Spaghettini. **Jill Norman**, *Winter Food* (Kyle Cathie): © p118 Spiced pumpkin soup; p133 Oysters; p155 Spiced syllabub. **Jane Cumberbatch**, Designer (www.sierrarica.com): © p120 Tomato, chestnut and chorizo soup; p184 Chestnut stuffing; p198 Chestnut and chocolate truffles. **Antonio Carluccio** (www.carluccios.com), *Italia* (Quadrille): © p123 Fresh porcini. **Thierry Boué**, Bliss Spas: © p124 Pear, Parmesan and truffle salad. **Serena Bass**, New York caterer: © p125 Sweet potato latkes. **Clarissa Dickson Wright**, *The Game Cookbook* (Kyle Cathie): © p126 Carpaccio of grouse; p135 Saddle of fallow deer. **Detmar Blow**, Blow de la Barra Gallery, London: © p129 Cheddar and tarragon soufflé. **Gordon Ramsay**, *Recipes from a *** Chef* (Quadrille): © p134 Steak. **Krug Champagne** (www.krug.com): © p142 Potée Champenoise; p158 Tarte aux raisins. **Darina Allen**, *Irish Traditional Cooking* (Kyle Cathie), Ballymaloe Cookery School, Cork, Eire (www.ballymaloe.ie): © p146 Scallion champ; p167 Cockley soup; p203 White soda bread. **Myrtle Allen**, *The Ballymaloe Cookbook* (Methuen): © p146 Colcannon. **Nigel Slater**, *Real Food and Appetite* (Fourth Estate): © p148 Roast potatoes; p166 A fast, warming bowl of soup. **Alastair Hendy**, (www.alastairhendy.com): © p148 Pan-roast tomatoes; p157 Windfall toffee apples. **Ben Murray** (www.goodwebsite.co.uk): © p157 Apple and blueberry crumble; p161 Cheese straws; p171 Pork belly. **Chantal Coady**, Rococo Chocolates, London (www.rococochocolates.com): © p161 Chocolate brownies. **Richard Allen**, Harvey Nichols, Leeds (www.harveynichols.com): © p162 Apple and walnut cake. **Fortunes**, Fortunes Kippers, Whitby: © p170 Fortune's kipper paté. **Ranald Macdonald**, Boisdale Restaurants (www.boisdale.co.uk): © p173 Venison Napoleon. **Madhur Jaffrey**, *The Essential Madhur Jaffrey* (Ebury Press): © p177 Koftas. **Tom Norrington Davies**, *Just Like Mother Used to Make* (Cassell): © p181 Liver and bacon. **Elizabeth David**, *Elizabeth David's Christmas* (Penguin): © p194 Plum pudding. **Shaun Hill**, *How to Cook Better* (Mitchell Beazley): © p196 Rhubarb tart with ginger custard. **Claudia Roden**, *Arabesque: A Taste of Morocco, Turkey and Lebanon* (Penguin): © p198 Chocolate cake. **Dan Lepard**, *The Handmade Loaf* (Mitchell Beazley), (www.danlepard.com): © p200 Lentil rolls.

The Daily Telegraph has made every effort to obtain permissions and assign the correct copyright to all contributors and apologises for any unintentional omissions or errors.

Photographers' credits

© Edmund Barr, p77; © Luisa Beccaria, p6; © Martin Brigdale, p11; © David Crookes, p32, 116, 138, 140, 182; © Suki Dhanda p163; © Getty Images, p2; © Toby Glanville, p41, 94, 144; © Philip Lee Harvey, p82–3, 172, 173, 175; © Alastair Hendy, p149, 156; © Pal Hermansen, p164; © Adrian Houston, p14, 15, 18–19; © Ditte Isager, p8, 88, 92, 143, 169; © iStockphoto, p26-27; © Kalpesh Lathigra, p176; © Steve Lee, p50, 185; © Dan Lepard, p201 (reprinted by permission of Mitchell Beazley); © Lisa Linder, p21, 24, 42, 47, 52, 57, 59, 71, 78 (reprinted by permission of Conran Octopus), 91, 98 (reprinted by permission of Conran Octopus), 101, 105, 109, 160, 195; © David Loftus. All rights reserved, p34, 137; © Jason Lowe, p22, 29, 30–31, 45, 58, 73, 154, 199; © Stefano Massimo, p131; © James Merrell, p114; © nagelestock-com/Alamy, p54; © Cheryl Newman, p127, 132, 159; © Niels-DK/Alamy, p119; ©Michael Paul, p153; © Damien Russell, p39, 191 © Red Saunders, p122; © Matthew Septimus, p51 (reprinted by permission of Bloomsbury USA); © Howard Sooley, p192; © Pia Tryde, p68; ©Patrice de Villiers, p110; © Jenny Zarins, p12, 62–63, 66, 74, 87.